MW01491633

CELEBRATIONS & OBSERVANCES

of the Church Year

CELEBRATIONS & OBSERVANCES

of the Church Year

Leading Meaningful Services from Advent to All Saints' Day

Gary Lee Waller

BEACON HILL PRESS
OF KANSAS CITY

Copyright 2009 by Gary Lee Waller and Beacon Hill Press of Kansas City

ISBN 978-0-8341-2433-2

Printed in the
United States of America

Cover Design: J.R. Caines
Interior Design: Sharon Page

Permission is granted upon purchase to make copies of the "Advent Family Worship Guide" (Appendix 2) for noncommercial use within the local church.

All Scripture quotations not otherwise designated are from the *Holy Bible, New International Version®* (NIV®). Copyright © 1973, 1978, 1984 by International Bible Society. Used by permission of Zondervan Publishing House. All rights reserved.

Scripture quotations marked KJV are from the King James Version of the Bible.

The following copyrighted versions of the Bible are used by permission:

Scripture quotations marked CEV are from the *Contemporary English Version* (CEV). Copyright © by American Bible Society, 1991, 1992.

Scripture quotations marked ESV are from *The Holy Bible, English Standard Version®* (ESV), copyright © 2001 by Crossway Bibles, a publishing ministry of Good News Publishers. All rights reserved.

Scripture quotations marked NASB are from the *New American Standard Bible®* (NASB®), © copyright The Lockman Foundation 1960, 1962, 1963, 1968, 1971, 1972, 1973, 1975, 1977, 1995.

Scripture quotations marked NKJV are from the *New King James Version* (NKJV). Copyright © 1979, 1980, 1982 Thomas Nelson, Inc.

Scripture quotations marked TM are from *The Message* (TM). Copyright © 1993, 1994, 1995, 1996, 2000, 2001, 2002. Used by permission of NavPress Publishing Group.

Library of Congress Cataloging-in-Publication Data

Waller, Gary Lee, 1950-
   Celebrations and observances of the church year : leading meaningful services from Advent to All Saints' Day / Gary Lee Waller.
      p. cm.
   Includes bibliographical references.
   ISBN 978-0-8341-2433-2 (pbk.)
   1. Church year. I. Title.
   BV30.W275 2009
   263'.9—dc22

                                                                        2008045382

10 9 8 7 6 5 4 3 2 1

CONTENTS

ACKNOWLEDGMENTS

I would like to acknowledge and sincerely thank the many people who have been involved in the creation of this book.

I offer my deepest gratitude and admiration to my wife, Ann, for her love, patience, and support during our years of ministry together. As wife to a workaholic pastor and university professor she has put up with late nights, absenteeism, and feelings of being second fiddle. Her encouragement has ultimately been the catalyst to complete this work.

I also give thanks

to Rob Robinson. Rob and his family have been members of two congregations where I have served as a pastor. Rob is an able churchman whose deep love for Jesus, his family, and others shines through his life. He spent many hours researching for this manuscript, making an indispensable contribution. Rob, a schoolteacher for a number of years, has taught both at the junior high and elementary levels. He has authored two children's books, two other works of fiction, as well as many poems and short stories.

to the late Rev. W. Don Adams I owe a debt for the poems he gave to me to publish so many years ago. Don was a pastor of small churches, a church builder, and a devoted follower of Jesus. He loved to write poetry, and he entrusted me with these poems as the fruit of his years of labor. He and his wife, Fern, were members of our congregation in Kent, Washington, and he was a great supporter of this fellow Montanan.

to my friends Ryan Ketchum, Johnny Hampton, Todd McArthur, Chad Johnson, and Mike Kipp, who have listened to me, inspired me, and challenged me to think deeply and creatively about worship.

to Mike Wiebe, Craig Morton, Gene Lubiens, and Ryan Roberts, who have read the manuscript and given me valuable insight and critique.

to Dr. William Greathouse, who read the manuscript and encouraged me to pursue publication and advocated for its publication.

to the congregations of Kent Church of the Nazarene, Enumclaw Church of the Nazarene, Nampa First Church of the Nazarene, Nampa College Church of the Nazarene, and Nampa Fairview Church of the Nazarene, who have used the "Advent Family Worship Guide" (see Appendix 2), listened to my sermons about the church year, and encouraged me to follow through with this project.

CELEBRATIONS
& OBSERVANCES

of the Church Year

INTRODUCTION

In picking up this book, a person might ask, "Who needs another book on worship? Aren't there enough books on the church year?" While countless books feature the church year, my hope is that this particular work will appeal to the pastor and worship leader who have not discovered the church year's value and rich heritage. This work was designed to inspire and guide those in nonliturgical free churches, as well as those who identify with postmodernism and are looking for a substantial way to enhance their worship.

Moreover, this book is neither a study of the theory of worship nor is it about worship styles. It is instead a bridge or tool that any church can use, regardless of its style of worship. Barry Liesch says, "Nothing short of a revolution in worship styles is sweeping across North America. Pastors, worship leaders, and congregations face new and powerful forces of change—forces that bring renewal to some churches and fear to others."[1] Because of this revolution, some may think that changing the style of worship will resuscitate a dying church. This book does not argue that point but instead maintains the belief that the church year can provide a foundation from which to teach and disciple a congregation. My hope is that as individuals and congregations better understand the historical themes and celebrations surrounding worship, this discovery will enrich their worship. In that sense this book is a work of theology. When a person enters into worship, a dialogue centered on what he or she believes and says about God begins, and that's what makes this a book about Christian faith.

Christian faith is often taught through theology courses, biblical studies, evangelism, or preaching. For many, the Bible is a guidebook of moral behavior or a set of beliefs that control thoughts and actions, but a growing number of biblical scholars and theologians are emphasizing the importance of seeing the Bible as an overarching story. They assert that the main task of *theology* is to unravel and make sense of the biblical story. Michael Lodahl reminds us, "Human beings are storytellers. We love to tell stories, and we love to listen to them. We tend to understand our own individual lives in terms of a story."[2] The Christian, or church, year is a way to retell the story of Jesus Christ as the central focus of the gathered church. Christians celebrate the story by marking those particular events in which God's saving purposes were made known. Different aspects of God's redemptive plan are demonstrated through each major event or celebration. Just as the regular calendar is marked by seasons that prescribe secular interests, the Christian year has seasons that annually inspire moods for worship.

During many of my years in pastoral ministry, I failed to mine the riches of the church year for sermons, worship, and celebrations. The topic of the church year was not part of my training in college or seminary, but in recent years I have found it meaningful to organize worship, preaching, and teaching around such a calendar. I have received an overwhelming response from congregations who have been exposed to the richness of the traditions, liturgy, and faith that characterize the calendar's special days of celebration.

This response is what inspired me to write this book. I saw the impact these practices had upon the congregations I had the privilege to lead, and I was thrilled at the way they so readily hungered for something—a symbol or a memory—that would inspire them to know and seek God. It is my hope and prayer that worship leaders, pastors, and others directing worship will find this a rich tool as they lead people in worship, word, and sacrament.

The Christian Year

The Christian year acts as a guide to spirituality and a textbook of theology. Its roots are found in God's initial covenant with Israel. When God gave Israel the Law, as recorded in the first five books of the Bible, He established a calendar to mark certain days for spiritual observances. The heart of this calendar was the Sabbath (Hebrew for "rest"). Because God had created the world in six days and rested on the seventh, He commanded Israel also to rest on the seventh. In addition to this weekly observance, God gave Israel a number of other observances or festivals to remember throughout the year. Some of these included Passover, Pentecost, the Feast of Tabernacles, and the Day of Atonement. These festivals reminded the children of Israel of their roots, their salvation history, and their God; they provided a natural rhythm for memory and celebration.

What was true for Israel holds true for the Christian Church. Humans enjoy celebrations: birthdays, wedding anniversaries, and holidays that mark special days. Our human psychological makeup naturally calls us to remember special days as opportunities to celebrate life and to honor the past. People associate the return of dates and seasons with remembering. Around these seasonal memories, the early Christians created another rhythm, the annual liturgical cycle. (Liturgy simply refers to sequence, order, or form.) The rhythm of the liturgical seasons reflects the rhythm of life with its celebrations of anniversaries and its seasons of growth and maturing.

While Jewish celebrations revolve around the Exodus from Egypt and other historical events such as Hanukkah, the Christian year focuses on the life and ministry of Jesus. It is a journey that follows the life of Christ and invites the worshipper to remember and sense the significance of dozens of scriptural events, persons, and images. The Christian year has developed through centuries of practice. At times it has been changed or abbreviated in order to focus even more clearly on the person and work of Christ, but it has always challenged

Christian worshippers to deepen their understanding of their faith, to marvel at the great power and love of God as shown in Jesus Christ, and to celebrate their place in the Body of Christ. The changing seasons of the year provide recurring opportunities to celebrate the Christian faith in worship.

The Roman Catholic Church's *Constitution on the Sacred Liturgy* captures the importance of celebrating the church year:

> The Church is conscious that it must celebrate the saving work of the divine Bridegroom by devoutly recalling it on certain days throughout the course of the year. Every week, on the day which the Church has called the Lord's Day [Sunday], it keeps the memory of the Lord's resurrection, which it also celebrates once in the year, together with his blessed passion, in the most solemn festival of Easter.

> Within the cycle of a year, moreover, the Church unfolds the whole mystery of Christ, from his incarnation and birth until his ascension, the day of Pentecost, and the expectation of blessed hope and of the Lord's return.

> Recalling thus the mysteries of redemption, the Church opens to the faithful the riches of the Lord's powers and merits, so that these are in some way made present in every age in order that the faithful may lay hold on them and be filled with saving grace.[3]

Some churches in the Protestant tradition do not celebrate the various seasons of the church year beyond Christmas and Easter in any deliberate or sustained way; however, the observance of the seasons of the church year has a long history in the life of the Christian faith. When most of the people in the church were poor and had no access to education, the church festivals and seasons provided a vehicle for teaching the story of God and His actions in human history. According to Dennis Bratcher:

> As a congregation moves through the church calendar, they

are presented in an organized way with the opportunity to talk about, reflect upon, and respond to the entire range of faith confessions that lie at the heart of the Christian Faith. This is important, not only for the vitality of the whole community, but especially for children to become aware in the context of community celebration those things that are essential to their Faith (Deut 6:20-25).[4]

The Early Church believed that the meaning of Christian time was interpreted through the death and resurrection of Jesus. With the Resurrection at the center of Christian worship, each Sunday was considered a "mini-Easter," a weekly celebration of Christ being raised from the dead. The Christian year was a vital part of worship until the Reformation, when Protestants abandoned much of these ideas because of the abuses attached to the various celebrations in the late medieval period. The Roman Catholic Church had connected every day of the year with a saint. These days and feasts tended to overshadow the Christ event, which was to be the focus of Christian worship. This loss of focus created a theological rift because the focal point and source of the Christian year is the death and resurrection of Christ.

Following the church year is more than simply marking time on calendars or making notes of recognition in church bulletins. Every effort should be made to use the different aspects of the church year as an opportunity to tell the story of God's redemptive work in the world. Biblical scholar N. T. Wright makes this very point:

> Many churches have relied almost solely on the spoken word to carry the burden of proclamation. However, even in the Old Testament the services of worship involved all of the senses: sight, smell, taste, touch, as well as hearing. Modern learning theory also indicates that the more senses are involved in an experience, the more impact it makes, especially for children. This suggests that the worship experience should be concerned with more than just preaching and music.[5]

The particular celebrations that revolve around these special days teach and encourage Christians through preaching, music, colors, banners, scripture reading, drama, and the sacraments. The exact times and dates of the seasons, and even some of the seasons themselves, differ within various traditions, especially between the Western Roman and the Eastern Orthodox traditions. There are several reasons for this dating issue: various historical emphases, different ways of calculating the days, and the use of different calendars. The dates chosen within this document align closely with the modern Roman calendar and the Revised Common Lectionary. Although one can find richness from a study of the Eastern Orthodox traditions and reasons for their celebrations, for the purposes of this reflection they will not be included.

An Overview

Unlike most conventional calendars, the Christian calendar does not begin with January 1. Instead, the church year begins with the season of Advent and ends with Christ the King Sunday. The Christian calendar is organized around three major centers of sacred time: the Christmas Cycle with Advent, Christmas, and Epiphany; the Easter Cycle with Lent, Holy Week, Easter, and the Day of Pentecost; and the Church Cycle, which is known as the Sundays after Pentecost or Ordinary Time. See chart below:

The Christmas Cycle
    ADVENT SEASON
    The Advent season starts four Sundays before Christmas and ends the Sunday prior to Christmas Day. When the fourth Sunday of Advent coincides with Christmas Eve, Sunday morning worship is in the Advent season and the afternoon/evening worship is in the Christmas season.

    CHRISTMAS SEASON
    The Nativity of Our Lord: Christmas Eve (December 24) and Christmas Day (December 25)

The Naming (and Circumcision) of Jesus

Epiphany (January 6; the Sunday closest to January 6 could be the celebration of Epiphany.)

SEASON AFTER EPIPHANY

First Sunday after Epiphany—Baptism of the Lord (Sunday closest to January 13)

Sundays after Epiphany until Transfiguration

Transfiguration Sunday (Sunday closest to February 10, Sunday before Ash Wednesday)

Valentine's Day—February 14, The Story of St. Valentine (Although not a part of the traditional church calendar, this holiday has become important to the church in celebrating love. It could be celebrated on the Sunday following Transfiguration.)

The Easter Cycle

LENTEN SEASON

Ash Wednesday (starts 46 days before Easter)

Lent: There are five Sundays of Lent

Holy Week (week prior to Easter)

Palm (Passion) Sunday

Monday in Holy Week

Tuesday in Holy Week

Wednesday in Holy Week—foot washing or holy Communion

Maundy (Holy) Thursday—holy Communion, foot washing, and/or Tenebrae

Good Friday—Tenebrae or Good Friday Service

EASTER SEASON

The Great Paschal Vigil (Saturday night before Easter Sunday)

Easter Sunday—the celebration of the resurrection of Jesus

Holy Humor Sunday—the joke is on Satan

Ascension Day—40 days after Easter (if not celebrated on Thursday, this festival may be moved to the seventh Sunday of Easter)

Pentecost Sunday—50 days after Easter

The Church Cycle
    AFTER PENTECOST (Ordinary Time—counted from first Sunday af-
        ter Pentecost to Christ the King Sunday)
    Trinity Sunday (first Sunday after Pentecost)
    Reformation Sunday (Sunday nearest October 31)
    All Hallows Eve (October 31)
    All Saints' Day (November 1)
    Christ the King Sunday—last Sunday of the church year
(The above are all explained more fully in the rest of the book.)

Colors of the Church Year

The Church has used colors for centuries to assist in celebrating the seasons of the church year. The various colors provide a visual context for worship. Different colors are associated with different seasons. The changing colors of the coverings (paraments) on table/altar and pulpit, and the pastoral attire (vestments) all provide visual interest and teaching for the seasons. Some churches do not use pulpit paraments or pastoral vestments. In that case, other ways of displaying the colors for the season can be creatively explored, such as banners and drapes. Below are the recommended colors:

- **Advent.** Blue symbolizes preparation and hope for Christ's coming; it is also the color of Mary. Violet expresses the royalty of Christ, fulfilling the prophecies of the coming Messiah. If violet is used during Advent, the color should be different from the violet of Lent, since the seasons are different.

- **Christmas.** White is used for festivals of Christ and expresses gladness, joy, and light.

- **After Epiphany.** Green expresses the ongoing eternal nature of growth.

- **Lent.** Black (on Ash Wednesday) and violet express the solemnity of Lent and its penitential nature.

- **Holy Week.** Scarlet is used as the color of the blood of Christ. Black is also used to express the somber nature of Good Friday.

Use white or scarlet for Maundy Thursday. Since it is traditional to strip the table/altar of all colors at the end of the Maundy Thursday worship, Good Friday and Holy Saturday have no color.

- **Easter.** White expresses the joy of the season.
- **Pentecost Sunday.** Red symbolizes fire and the coming of the Holy Spirit.
- **Trinity.** White.
- **After Pentecost.** Green expresses the ongoing work of God.
- **All Saints' Day.** Since this day is considered a "feast of the church" by commemorating all "saints" (Paul's definition), the color is white.
- **Christ the King Sunday.** White expresses the celebratory nature of this day.

Secular Days

What about those holidays that have found their way into the life of the Church and the celebration of the life of Christ? What about Mother's and Father's days, Thanksgiving, or other secular holidays of note? Churches in North America have celebrated these special days for years. These celebrations provide an opportunity for the preacher to focus on a particular issue or group of people to be honored, challenged, or encouraged. One must make sure not to make these central to the Christian calendar. These secular days are to be secondary when they conflict with a significant day of the church year.

The Role of the Worship Leader

The worship leader plays an instrumental role as he or she guides the congregation in observance of these special celebrations. It is imperative that the worship leader assume the role of teacher and director of congregational worship and not simply that of music director. Therefore it is imperative that worship leaders educate themselves regarding the Christian calendar, discovering its history, theology, and importance. The worship leader is not the star or performer but the one who calls the congregation to open their hearts in worship. The Greek word for *worship* is variously translated "to bow," "to do reverence to," "to kiss the hand of," or other expressions that indicate an acknowledgment of the presence of someone great. The worship leader in conjunction with the preaching pastor should organize worship services that lead people into the presence of God.

The Role of Scripture

Scripture plays a foundational role in all of worship and particularly in the Christian calendar. It is to be read during the worship services and provides the background and basis for the celebrations. The lectionary may be used to provide the scriptural foundation for the church year celebrations, or pastors and worship leaders can choose their own biblical passages to be used in public reading. It is imperative that scriptures be read publicly, for lives are changed and impacted by their reading. Public scripture reading should not only be relegated to special days but also have a significant place every time people gather.

The Lectionary

Use of the Christian calendar may frustrate a pastor or worship leader because finding suitable Scripture readings, preaching texts, and worship themes may prove formidable. One responsibility of the pastoral office is to provide meaningful sermons Sunday after Sunday. The Christian calendar helps with the theme, but what about appropriate texts for preaching? One of the things that a thoughtful pastor can do is to use a lectionary. A lectionary is simply a list of Bible passages for reading, study, or preaching in services of worship. Generally, a lectionary can include weekday readings, but the term is more commonly applied to the Scripture readings for Sundays and holidays (holy days).

Roman Catholics and most mainline Protestants follow a three-year shared lectionary known as the Revised Common Lectionary.

Lists of readings similar to contemporary lectionaries started to appear in the second century when Christians began their various worship celebrations by reading the Word of God, a practice that was grounded in Jewish synagogue worship. This custom of reading the Law and the Prophets, the letters of Paul, and the stories about Jesus resulted in the formation of the Old and New Testament canons. "And on the day called Sunday, all who live in cities or in the country gather together to one place, and the memoirs of the apostles or the writings of the prophets are read, as long as time permits; then, when the reader has ceased, the president verbally instructs, and exhorts to the imitation of these good things."[6]

When a pastor or worship leader first encounters the lectionary, it may seem overwhelming or difficult. Pastors often ask, "How does one study for a sermon, given the variety of scriptures listed to be read in each service?" There are several options, all of which could be employed with great success over the course of the church year. A pastor may choose to

- Find a common theme among the scriptures and weave the sermon around this theme.
- Select one of the passages from the lectionary readings and focus on it for that particular Sunday. It is important that the overall theme be understood and communicated or else the reading of the remaining scripture passages may be confusing for the congregation.
- Pick a couple of the given passages that fit together well and develop the sermon around them. Also, keep in mind the theme of all.

It is not always easy to create a sermon from the passages provided in the lectionary readings. Some seem dark and difficult, but perseverance will usually prove fruitful. As in all preaching, the Holy

Spirit will actively guide the preacher through the texts. The discipline of studying the Scriptures daily and reflecting upon the preacher's context will help the sermon move forward. Charles Spurgeon, the great British pastor, often exhorted preachers to keep a balance between the text of Scripture and the context of the people while preparing sermons.

In many evangelical churches pastors prepare annual preaching schedules around books of the Bible, topical and biblical themes, and issues and concerns of their congregations. Pastors need not abandon this pattern of preaching but may insert the special celebration days as they arise within the church year. However, I encourage pastors to try the lectionary for one year. It requires a pastor to cover all or most of the great themes of Scripture, relies significantly upon the Holy Spirit to provide the connections, and forces pastors to not produce last-minute wonders or constantly repeat certain favorite themes. Most importantly it encourages pastors to pursue a life of disciplined study. The primary benefit of using the lectionary is the public reading of Scripture.

Many churches today claim reliance upon the Bible as the source of doctrine and life. However, few actually read large portions of Scripture during their worship gatherings, relying instead upon Bible study groups to do this work. Scripture reading in many churches only occurs when the pastor reads the scripture passage related to the sermon. James Smart says, "The Bible is a book to be studied by the Christian community. Make it primarily devotional literature for private use and no longer is it given the attention it requires," neither does it become the authoritative guide for the Church but a source of "individualistic interpretation and thereby silenced at the most incisive points of its message."[7] Using the lectionary enables the church to hear a larger portion of the Bible and to see its overarching themes. Over the course of the cycles of the lectionary all of the main themes and ideas of Scripture will be covered.

The Revised Common Lectionary[8] is divided into three-year cycles. The three-year Sunday cycle is based upon the three synoptic Gospels: Matthew (Year A), Mark (Year B), and Luke (Year C). Selections from the Gospel of John are inserted at different times in all three cycles. Each Sunday contains an Old Testament reading, which is chosen because of its connection with that Sunday's Gospel. Other readings include excerpts from the Epistles and Acts of the Apostles. A psalm for each Sunday is also appointed for responsive reading or singing/chanting. Each Sunday usually has four readings. During the "green season" of Ordinary Time, choices are provided that enable the pastor to read the Old Testament readings sequentially.

The Church Year and the Lectionary Readings begin with Advent. Below are the dates for the three-year lectionary cycle:

Year A: 2001-2, 2004-5, 2007-8

Year B: 2002-3, 2005-6, 2008-9

Year C: 2003-4, 2006-7, 2009-10

(The following is an example of use of the lectionary in worship.)

The Liturgy of the Word includes
The First Reading
(Usually taken from the Old Testament or the Acts of the Apostles)

The Responsorial Psalm

The Second Reading
(Usually taken from the New Testament Epistles)

The Gospel Reading
These readings would be sequenced in a manner that best prepares the congregation for the lesson of the day. They are placed in appropriate places between other parts of the liturgy for the day.

How to Use the Church Year as a Resource

The remaining chapters will expand upon the sections briefly outlined above. Practical tools and hands-on materials will be offered as examples for use in worship services, families, and small groups. It is my hope that as you use this work as a resource, it will inspire you to seek other resources to enrich and deepen your understanding of these grand celebrations of the church year.

THE CHRISTMAS CYCLE

Today in the town of David

a Savior has been born to you;

he is Christ the Lord.

—Luke 2:11

1

THE ADVENT SEASON

Advent—What Is It?

Advent is the time of preparation before the celebration of the birth of Christ. The word *advent* is from the Latin word *adventus*, which means "coming," referring to the coming birth of Jesus. Advent comprises the four Sundays preceding Christmas and signals the start of the Christian year. Historically, Advent focused on the second coming of Jesus and thus was the season concluding the Christian year. Today Advent encompasses both themes: the expectation of the second coming of Christ and the beginning of the Christian year inaugurated by the hope of Christ's birth.

Advent was not celebrated until the fourth century following the introduction of Christmas to the Christian calendar. This season originated as a period during which converts prepared themselves for baptism through instruction, prayer, fasting, and reflection, much like Lent. The length of Advent varied from three days to six weeks, in observance of the approximate length of time that Jesus spent in the wilderness preparing for His ministry.

Advent remains a time of preparation, prayer, joy, and happiness as a celebration and remembrance of the first Advent of Jesus, the Incarnate One. Even though the modern lectionaries focus the Advent texts on the preparation for Christ's birth, rather than on His second coming, preachers should not forget Advent's somber prophetic tone. Some of the lectionary readings for Advent reflect this by including a strong note of accountability and judgment of sin.

These readings remind us of the role of the King who comes to rule, save, and judge the world.

Advent is a rich mix of politics, prophecy, prayer, and perseverance. It is a season to prepare hearts to remember what God has done in Jesus and to anticipate what is to come. The challenge of Advent is to live in the present, to embrace the present, to celebrate the present, but to also look forward to God's ultimate redemption. The Christian task is not simply to wait white-robed for the soon coming Jesus but rather to participate in God's involvement and presence throughout all ages, including the present kingdom of God. Advent prompts us to ask the question, "God, I don't know what You are doing today, but I want to be part of it." The challenge and joy of Advent is preparation for the advent of Christ into our world, which not only happened over two millennia ago but also is happening daily as we live as "Advent people," anticipating His daily presence and His future appearing.

It is important to remember that the seasons of Advent and Christmas are different. Some traditions do not sing Christmas songs during Advent but focus primarily on preparation for the birth of the Christ child. Since the themes of expectation and longing are key to the Advent season, it is important to focus on preparation. Singing a song such as "Joy to the World" seems to be a bit out of sequence. "O Come, O Come, Emmanuel" is much more appropriate for this season. It focuses on the expectation and anticipation of the coming birth of the Promised One. Advent prepares us for the celebration of Christmas much like the season of Lent prepares us for Easter. Other traditions blend the two themes so as to allow congregants to remember and celebrate both aspects of the Advent season.

The Advent Wreath

One way to mark these weeks of preparation is with an Advent wreath, which can be created both at home and at church. The specific origins of the Advent wreath are not known, but historians be-lieve it began centuries ago in Eastern Europe, perhaps in Germany. The wreath is made with pine boughs and evergreens to symbolize everlasting life, the gift Messiah Jesus brought into the world. The circle represents the eternal nature of God.

The Symbols of the Advent Wreath

The purpose of the wreath is to deepen our understanding of Christmas.

1. The base of the wreath is covered with green—the color green testifies to the continuation of life in Christ.

2. The circular base represents life without end—eternal life.

3. The candles signify God's Son as the Light of the World.

There are five candles in all. The first, second, and fourth candles are violet or purple, the royal color, to symbolize our penitence and preparation. The third candle is pink to symbolize joy and happiness, the symbol of hope. In the center of the wreath is the white candle, which represents Christ. White refers to the Lord's purity and perfec-tion. These candles represent the four Sundays preceding the Nativi-ty, one candle being lit each Sunday, with the white candle at the wreath's center being lit on Christmas Eve. All red or all blue or all white candles may be substituted if desired.

How to Make an Advent Wreath

The wreath should be in the form of a circle. The base of the wreath can be made from Styrofoam, wire, or wood. Anchor the can-dleholders securely in the base.

Cover the base with greenery. If live evergreens are used, make sure to protect them from fire. Spraying them with fire retardant is an excellent precaution and will ease your mind.

The Advent Candles

Each candle communicates a particular weekly Advent theme. There are several ways of naming or describing the weekly themes represented by the candles. The following is the one I prefer, but there are other ways of viewing the weekly progression.

- The first candle symbolizes *Prophecy,* which calls attention to the prophecies of the coming Savior. It calls us to prepare for Christmas by prayerfully humbling ourselves before God.
- The second candle represents *Bethlehem,* the lowly birthplace of our Savior.
- The third candle is the *Shepherd* candle, colored pink to represent joy and celebration. The shepherds remind us that we share in the joy of Jesus' birth.
- The fourth candle is the *Angel* candle, which reminds us of the messengers who came to proclaim Christ's birth.
- The fifth candle is the *Christ* candle that symbolizes Christ's presence in our world.

Robert Webber argues that "the colors of the candles can celebrate the twin themes of Advent—preparation and joy. Since preparation is solemn and even penitential, the first, second, and fourth candles should be dark blue or purple. The third candle, which symbolizes the joy of anticipation, is always rose-colored. And the Christ candle is white, the symbol of festivity."[1] The candles of the Advent wreath provide a way of counting down the days until Christmas. The scriptures that accompany each theme cover the entire Advent story.

If December 24 is a Sunday, the morning worship service is considered the fourth Sunday in Advent and the late afternoon or evening worship is Christmas Eve.

The Five Candles and Their Symbolism

1. First Candle: First Sunday in Advent
   Color: Purple
   Story: Prophecy
   Theme: Hope
   Alternate Theme: Vigilant waiting for the birth of Christ

---

2. Second Candle: Second Sunday in Advent
   Color: Purple
   Story: Bethlehem
   Theme: Peace
   Alternate Theme: Personal preparation for the birth of Christ
3. Third Candle: Third Sunday in Advent
   Color: Pink
   Story: Shepherds
   Theme: Joy
   Alternate Theme: The joy of our waiting
4. Fourth Candle: Fourth Sunday in Advent
   Color: Purple
   Story: Angels
   Theme: Love
   Alternate Theme: The incarnation of the Word in the womb of the
      Virgin Mary
5. Center Candle: Christmas Day
   Color: White
   Theme: Christmas
   Alternate Theme: The birth of the Savior[2]

Practical Ideas for Use of the Wreath

Using the wreath for public worship during the Sundays of Advent. It is appropriate to have a short candlelighting ceremony during each of the four worship services in Advent. Each week an individual or group can begin by lighting the candles that were lit the week(s) previously, naming them as they do. In this way they remind the congregation of the meaning of the previous candles. Participants then light the candle for the present Sunday, read scripture connected with that Sunday's theme, and offer a simple prayer that reminds the congregation of the season. (A suggested script is provided in Appendix 1 for each of these presentations, or participants can be encouraged to write their own scripts.)

Using the wreath for public worship on Christmas Eve or

Christmas Day. Light the four candles in the order you lit them before, again naming them and explaining the significance each one represents. Light the center candle with a short presentation or reading. If your church does not have a Christmas Day service, it would be appropriate to light the Christ candle during the Christmas Eve service.

Using the wreath for private home devotions. Christian rituals are of great importance in the character formation of children. Family rituals will help develop Christian attitudes, habits, and values as children grow and ultimately form their own families. These rituals also create strong ties that help to weave the family together. Gathering the family each day during the Advent Season to light the candles on a family Advent wreath, sing, pray, study the ancient stories, and share ideas, thoughts, and insights of the season may be the most important gift you give your child. Christmas toys will break and clothes will soon be outgrown, but the gift of our time in preparing our hearts and those of our children will be long-lasting. (See the "Advent Family Worship Guide" in Appendix 2.)

Along with lighting an Advent wreath, another way a family can count down or celebrate the Advent season is to create an Advent calendar. Children create a calendar that has hidden windows over each date. As each day passes, the window coverings are removed and the picture or symbol narrates part of the story of Christmas. Advent calendars can also be purchased at Christian bookstores, online, or at some retail outlets. Another way to participate is to create a Jesse Tree. A Jesse Tree can either be a banner or a poster. Pictures, ornaments, or symbols are pinned to the tree as the story of the Incarnation is told. Several options for the ornaments as well as the stories of the Jesse Tree may be found on the Internet.

2

THE CHRISTMAS SEASON

Christmas is the most popular holiday of the year. It is a holiday replete with dreams of presents, candy, great food, family, and gaily decorated stores and homes, holiday music, and lots of laughter. Among many Christians the holiday is valued even more than the other most holy day of Christianity, Easter. Especially for the young, the story of Christmas with all the images of angels and a young mother, of shepherds and a stable, of wise men and King Herod makes the season captivating.

Christmas is the celebration of the birth of Jesus. He is the prophesied Messiah, the one born and anointed King of the Jews and of the world. The angel Gabriel broke the news to a young maiden of Nazareth by the name of Mary, stating that she was to be the mother of the Savior. Another dimension of Christmas is that it is the story of God's great love: "For God so loved the world that he gave his one and only son" (John 3:16).

Theologically, Christmas is the celebration of the incarnation of God in Jesus the Christ as the self-revelation of God to the world in human form for the reconciliation of humanity to himself. Paul says it best in Philippians: "[Jesus] had equal status with God but didn't think so much of himself that he had to cling to the advantages of that status no matter what. Not at all. When the time came, he set aside the privileges of deity and took on the status of a slave, became *human*! Having become human, he stayed human" (2:6-7, TM).

While we most often think about Christmas as a single day, the celebration is actually a season of the year, beginning with Christmas Eve (December 24) and ending with Epiphany (January 6), a period of 12 days. These days are called the 12 days of Christmas or the season of Christmas. Many people are familiar with the popular song "The Twelve Days of Christmas." There are several myths surrounding the origin of the song. Some claim that it was used as an early catechism to teach Protestant children the Christian faith. Others would dispute this; whatever your position, talking about the 12 days of Christmas is still a great opportunity to teach the season of Christmas. Often families reserve the giving of gifts to these 12 intervening days. A present or gift is given for each day.

The Hanging of the Greens

Some Christmas traditions begin in Advent. The hanging of the greens has become for many congregations a time to party and prepare for the holiday. This is a time that the community gathers to decorate the church with evergreen wreaths, boughs, or trees that help to symbolize the new and everlasting life brought through Jesus the Christ. Some congregations have a committee that does the decorating, while others have a "party" in which members come together to adorn the church.

Each of these misses a significant opportunity for education and worship. A special weekday service, the first Sunday evening of Advent or even the first Sunday morning of Advent, can be wonderful opportunities in which the church is decorated and the Advent wreath put in place. A hanging of the greens service gives opportunity to discuss the reason for Advent and Christmas celebrations, the significance of the colors and decorations of the season, and a retelling of wonderful stories in preparation for Christmas. This service is a time to reflect upon all the meaning that surrounds the holiday rather than just a one-time event. It is most often comprised of music, especially choir and handbells, and Scripture reading, along with an explanation of the various symbols surrounding the Christmas season as they are placed in the sanctuary. (An order of service as well as an explanation of the meaning of each component of the service is in Appendix 3.)

Christmas Eve Vespers

One of the most meaningful gathering times for churches and communities of faith is the Christmas Eve service. Traditionally, this was the night that the manger scene, the crèche, was displayed. It was also the night that the Christmas tree was trimmed, or decorated, and the star of Bethlehem put on top. The manger scene would not include the baby Jesus, since it would be added in the morning.

Where possible, candlelight services for Vespers create a meditative atmosphere that is a reminder that Jesus, the Light of the World, came into the world to save a lost humanity from eternal darkness (see John 1). If a congregation cannot have real candles, artificial candles and small lamps may be used. This service should begin in the early evening (around 5 P.M.) or late evening (around 10 P.M. or midnight), so families can attend the worship celebration as well as participate in traditional family events. (An order of service as well as a family guide is in Appendix 4.)

Christmas Day

Most families awaken early on Christmas Day to the laughter, squeals, and hubbub of hurriedly opened presents; others meet as communities of faith to celebrate the incarnation of the Savior of the world. Christmas Day worship services are special occasions that are celebrated by a variety of Christian traditions. The time of the service is often around 9 or 10 A.M. Families dress in their finest clothes in honor of the Savior's birth. The service is usually a short service filled with the singing of lots of Christmas hymns, the lighting of the Advent wreath, the reading of Christmas scriptures, a short homily, and a time of greeting and fellowship.

A Bit of Christmas History

The Early Church did not celebrate Christmas, since no one knew the exact date of the birth of the Christ child. The Bible gives no date, and the few clues present seem to point to a warmer time of year than December, especially since the shepherds are in the fields, "keeping watch over their flocks at night" (Luke 2:8). In Egypt the Early Church celebrated the birth of the Christ child on May 20. Most Christians were unsure if the birth of Jesus should be celebrated at all because birthdays, especially birthdays of kings, were pagan celebrations. Origen, an Early Church father and philosopher, wrote around A.D. 245 that celebrating Jesus' birthday would be sinful because it would be "as though He were King Pharaoh."

As time passed, more and more Christians wanted to mark the birth with some kind of ceremony. Three dates eventually became prominent: March 25, December 25, and January 6. January 6 was most popular, often as a dual observance of both His birth and baptism. It was called the Epiphany, or appearance, and by the third century many churches were observing Christ's birthday on that date. Clement of Alexandria, a Greek theologian, mentions that some Christians in Egypt had begun to commemorate Jesus' baptism on January 6.

By A.D. 354 the Roman church separated the birth from the baptism and proclaimed December 25 as the date to celebrate the birth of Jesus the Christ. The winter solstice, a pagan holiday called Saturnalias, was observed on December 25 on the Roman imperial calendar. Under Emperor Constantine Christianity became the official religion of the Roman Empire. Substituting a Christian holiday for a pagan one was one way to distance people from pagan customs. Furthermore, Jews had long celebrated Hanukkah, the festival of lights, around this time of year. Celebrating Christ's birth as the Light of the World fit perfectly in the darkness of winter. The Eastern Church's slow acceptance of Christmas on December 25 did not mean an abandonment of Epiphany. Epiphany became the day of the arrival of the wise men, which extended the Christmas season for 12 days.

In northern Europe pagan traditions included burning Yule logs in order to speed the sun to rebirth in the dark days of winter. They filled their houses with evergreens, mistletoe, holly, and ivy to defy winter's power to kill. The druids used mistletoe piled on altars and burned as a sacrifice in winter to bring back the sun. The plant symbolized hope and peace because enemies could meet under the mistletoe and embrace, dropping their weapons. With the coming of Christianity, and the hope of everlasting life through the Prince of Peace, the plant continued to have a place in Christmas. Holly also served as a symbol of Christmas, since legend holds that Jesus' crown of thorns had been fashioned from holly, whose berries, originally white, turned brilliant red when pressed on the Son of God's forehead.

In Europe, traditions of Christmas Eve worship included the lighting of a Yule log (observed above as originally a pagan tradition), the putting up and decorating of a tree, and making a manger scene with either living participants or small clay figures. In the 13th century Francis of Assisi first taught the people to remember the Babe in the manger by re-creating the simple stable scene on Christmas Eve, using real people and animals. The season gave people a reason to be glad in the midst of the cruelties of Northern European winters.

The tradition of the Christmas tree began when Boniface, an eighth-century English missionary, went to Germany and replaced the sacred oak of Odin with the fir tree, a symbol of the everlasting life given by Christ. Passion plays in Germany at Christmastime would retell biblical stories from Adam and Eve to Christ's resurrection and would use a fir tree hung with apples for the tree of the knowledge of good and evil. Martin Luther, walking home one clear winter evening, noticed the brilliant stars twinkling amid the ever-green trees. To recapture this loveliness for his family, he put a small tree in their home and placed lighted candles on the branches. Christmas trees were common by 1605 in Germany. A journal account of a citizen of Strasbourg notes: "At Christmas they set up fir trees in the parlors . . . and hang upon them roses cut from many-colored paper, apples, wafers, gilt-sugar" and these were known as the *Christ Baum*, or Christ tree.[1] The idea came to England in the 1840s when Queen Victoria married Prince Albert of Germany. The royal family's gigantic tree, bedecked with wax tapers and sweetmeats, set the trend for the rest of Great Britain. By 1860 glass baubles replaced the edible and handmade ornaments.

3

EPIPHANY

∞

Epiphany, along with Christmas and Easter, is one of the three oldest festival days of the Church. According to tradition it commemorates the first manifestation of Jesus Christ to the Gentiles. Strange visitors called magi in the biblical birth narratives, or the "three kings" in Christmas carols and artwork, were the first non-Jews to recognize that the Child born in Bethlehem was in fact the Savior of the world. Epiphany is a celebration of the coming of the wise men, who brought gifts to visit the Christ child. In their coming the wise men "reveal" Jesus to the world as Lord and King. Thus the day is now often observed as a time to highlight the mission of the Church.

The worship of Jesus by the magi corresponded to Simeon's blessing that this child Jesus would be "a light for revelation to the Gentiles," the Savior of all people (Luke 2:32). This was one of the first indications that Jesus came for all people of all nations, of all cultures, and that the work of God in the world would not be limited to only a few.

January 5—Twelfth Night or Epiphany Eve

In Western churches the evening preceding Epiphany is called Twelfth Night, which alludes to the 12 days between Christmas and Epiphany, allowing Christians to have a more reflective period in which they can contemplate the actual significance of Jesus Christ.

This period of 12 days allows an appropriate amount of time in which to probe to a deeper level of understanding. Thus Epiphany can be an occasion for illumination and discovery, a breakthrough moment in which those things that are most real (and thus most divine) in human life come shining through.

Customs of gift giving, an imitation of the wise men, were part of this night. Generally, men dressed as the three kings gave the gifts, but in Italy a curious folktale took over the custom. According to the story the three wise men were on their way from Jerusalem to Bethlehem when they passed an old woman cleaning her house. When she discovered where they were going, she wanted to go along and asked them to wait until she had finished cleaning. They told her they could not wait and she would have to follow after them. After finishing her cleaning she attempted to follow them, but they were out of sight. The legend holds that she still searches the world for the Christ child, leaving gifts in homes for children, hoping one home will be that of the Child. This custom migrated into Russia with the old woman known as Babushka.

January 6—Epiphany

The Feast of the Epiphany is older than the celebration of Christmas. It comes from the Greek word *epiphaneia*, literally it means appearing or brightness, referring to the times that Jesus' divine self was made manifest on earth. These times include when the wise men from the East came to worship Jesus, when the infant Jesus was dedicated in the Temple, when His cousin John baptized Him in the River Jordan and the Holy Spirit descended like a dove, and when Jesus performed His first miracle by changing water into wine at the wedding in Cana.

As early as the second century, Clement of Alexandria mentioned that a group of Christians kept an all-night vigil on January 6 to commemorate Jesus' baptism. The date, January 6, coincides with the date of the celebration in Egypt. The Early Church was combating the pagan festival to the sun god that the Egyptians celebrated on that date. The pagans held that the waters of the Nile were changed into wine by their god. Thus Jesus' recognition by kings, the dove descending at His baptism proclaiming Him Son of God, and the miracle of the changing of water into wine at the wedding in Cana of Galilee were all combined as a way to proclaim Jesus as more powerful than the gods of Egypt.

For many Protestant church traditions, the season of Epiphany extends from January 6 until Ash Wednesday, which begins the season of Lent leading to Easter. Depending on the timing of Easter, this longer period of Epiphany includes from four to nine Sundays. Other traditions, especially the Roman Catholic tradition, observe Epiphany as a single day, with the Sundays following Epiphany counted as Ordinary Time. In some Western traditions, the last Sunday of Epiphany is celebrated as Transfiguration Sunday. There are several themes that are an important part of the season of Epiphany: the coming of the three kings, the dedication of Jesus in the Temple, and the baptism of Jesus.

The Three Kings. The word *magi* comes from the old Persian *magu*, a hereditary class of scholar-priests. The Bible gives no number to them, but the mention of three unique gifts in Matthew's Gospel led to the assumption that there were three. By the sixth century Christians began the tradition of the three kings. By the ninth century the kings had names: Gaspar, king of Tarsus; Melchior, king of Arabia; and Balthazar, king of Sheba. The gifts they brought to the Christ child included gold, representing royalty; frankincense, symbolizing divinity; and myrrh, foreshadowing Christ's death because it was used in embalming. Christ became the representation of the gifts since He embodies all these symbols.

The celebration of the three kings is a time to remember that the wise men are the first Gentiles to worship the "newborn king." They reveal Jesus to the world as Lord and King. It is a great time to celebrate God's mission to the entire world.

The baptism of our Lord Jesus. The first Sunday after Epiphany is traditionally set aside to celebrate the baptism of Jesus in the Jordan River by John (as is the case in the Revised Common Lectionary). In the churches of the Eastern Orthodox tradition, the recognition of Christ's divinity occurs first at His baptism by John in the Jordan River. For these churches Jesus' baptism by John was the breakthrough moment because it was when He was recognized as the Son of God. The commemoration of the baptism, also called the Day of Lights or the Illumination of Jesus, was originally known as the birthday of Jesus because He was first born of the Virgin and then reborn in baptism. Thus, some refer to Christmas and Epiphany as the first and second Nativity, the second being Christ's manifestation to the world.

The dedication of the infant Jesus. On any Sunday following Epiphany the dedication of the infant Jesus in the Temple can be celebrated. It could be substituted for the baptism of Jesus. Luke 2:21-35 mentions this closing act of Christ being revealed to the nations. Mary and Joseph went to the Temple as the Law commanded. Mary had to be purified on the 40th day after giving birth to a son, and Jesus was to be presented to God with the sacrifice of two doves. As the young couple and the Child entered the Temple, they met an old, wise prophet named Simeon, who had waited his entire life for the promise God had given him. God had told him that he would one day see the Messiah, the Christ, the anointed Savior of Israel.

Upon seeing the holy family Simeon knew immediately that this Child was the one foretold to him. He took the Child from the astonished parents and, while holding Him in his arms, proclaimed a shocking blessing. Those observing this strange event probably shrugged it off as the ravings of an old man, since no priests or Levites rushed to see the baby and comment on His Messiahship, but

Jesus' parents were "amazed." Simeon's blessing was not fully joyous, since he told Mary, "A sword will pierce even your own soul" (Luke 2:35, NASB). Anna, a prophetess, a woman who had been given rare privileges in the male-dominated Temple culture of the time, was also listening. Some heads must have turned as she recognized the special Child. We can follow the example of Simeon and Anna, who point us to the next season in the Christian calendar, which reminds us of Jesus as the One who suffered for the sins of the world.

The remaining weeks of Epiphany provide opportunity to emphasize the ministry of Jesus, perhaps beginning with the wedding in Cana. Walking the congregation through the miracles, parables, or teachings of Jesus provides opportunities to focus on the life and ministry of Jesus leading up to Lent and the season of Easter.

As pastors lead their congregations into the New Year, a sermon and/or worship service around the theme of missions fits perfectly with the celebration of Epiphany. These themes of Scripture have been used for centuries to challenge the Church to be missional.

Transfiguration Sunday

Transfiguration Sunday is the last Sunday in the season of Christmas and Epiphany. Like the baptism, the Transfiguration marks a turning point in the ministry of Jesus. His face is now set toward the Cross, and He begins to speak of the suffering awaiting Him in Jerusalem. This day provides a great opportunity for pastors to discuss the two natures of Christ: His divinity and His humanity.

THE EASTER CYCLE

He is not here;

he has risen, just as he said.

Come and see the place where he lay.

—Matt. 28:6

4
THE LENTEN SEASON

∞

As early as the second century, the Church began observing a fast to prepare for the celebration of Easter known as Lent. Lent is a 40-day period before Easter that begins on Ash Wednesday. In the Western church Sundays are not counted in the 40 days because each Sunday is a weekly festival of the Resurrection. The Eastern church does not skip Sundays when calculating the length of Lent, so Lent always begins on "Clean Monday," the seventh Monday before Easter, and ends on the Friday before Palm Sunday, using the Eastern date for Easter. "All churches that have a continuous history extending before A.D. 1500 observe Lent. The ancient church that wrote, collected, canonized, and propagated the New Testament also observed Lent, believing it to be a commandment from the apostles."[1]

Lent is a season of soul-searching and repentance and a time of study and prayer. It is also a season for reflection and taking stock. Penitential prayer, fasting, and almsgiving have traditionally marked Lent. It was a time when the faithful rededicated themselves, repented, and committed to a renewed relationship with God. This season was also when new converts were instructed in the faith and prepared for baptism, when those who had been separated from the church would prepare to rejoin their communities of faith. The 40-day length of Lent is designed so that an individual Christian may imitate Jesus' withdrawal into the wilderness for 40 days.

Much discussion surrounds what constitutes a fast during Lent. Historically, people abstained from meat, but in modern times things like coffee, chocolate, alcohol, sugar, sweets, television, and sex have been objects of individual fasting covenants. Some traditions do not place as great an emphasis on fasting but rather focus on charitable deeds, especially helping those in physical need with food and clothing, or simply the giving of money to charities.

In the Western church, the Sundays of Lent are feast days. They are set aside to celebrate the sacrament of Holy Communion (the Eucharist or the Lord's Supper) and to remember the resurrection of Jesus.

Ideas for Worship

One idea is to use a rough wooden cross as a focal point for the season. The cross is usually erected in the sanctuary on Ash Wednesday as a visible symbol of the beginning of Lent and is usually draped

---

A Devotional Guide for the Lenten Season

This guide begins with the Sunday 40 days before Maundy (Holy) Thursday. Each week is based on a 40-day period found in the Bible, except for the sixth week that focuses on Palm Sunday and Holy Week.

First week—Moses' 40 days on Sinai to receive the tablets of the Law (Exod. 24:12-18).

Second week—Jonah's 40 days of preaching repentance to Nineveh (Jon. 3:1-10).

Third week—Goliath threatens Israel for 40 days, then God saves Israel through David (1 Sam. 17:1-52).

Fourth week—Elijah subsists 40 days on one cake and some water (1 Kings 19:1-8).

Fifth week—Jesus' 40-day fast in the desert (Matt. 4:1-11; Luke 4:1-13).

Sixth week—Palm Sunday.

Each Sunday can be marked with a candle. A traditional seven-candle church candelabra, or seven candleholders in a prominent place, works well.

in black on Good Friday. The same cross can also be part of the congregation's Easter celebration, draped in white and gold or covered with flowers.

One effective way to use the cross is as a prayer cross. A hammer, square nails, and small pieces of paper are placed near the cross. At a designated time of prayer on Sundays, people are invited to write their prayer requests on the paper and then nail them to the cross. The quiet time of prayer with only the sounds of the hammer and the nails can be a moving time for reflection on the meaning of Lent. The prayer requests can be removed and burned as part of a Tenebrae or stations of the cross service during Holy Week to symbolize releasing needs to God.

Ash Wednesday

Ash Wednesday, the seventh Wednesday before Easter Sunday, is the first day of the season of Lent. A meaningful service on Ash Wednesday can prepare the hearts of people for the Lenten season. The service could contain a call to worship, introduction of Ash Wednesday, singing of songs, reading of various Scriptures, and a short message and/or litany. Following the Ash Wednesday sermon, a mixture of oil and ashes can be placed on the foreheads of worshippers using the sign of the Cross as a symbol of mourning and sorrow over the consequences of sin and also as a sign of humility before God.

The palm branches from Palm Sunday are saved from the previous year and then burned into a fine ash. This preparation may happen on Shrove Tuesday, the day before Ash Wednesday, with a festive celebration prior to the disciplines of Lent. Traditionally, some congregations have served pancakes as a way to consume the remaining butter before the fast (butter was one food from which people abstained). The ashes are then mixed with olive oil to be used to anoint the foreheads of congregants. It is recommended that the mixture not be overly oily as it may run or drip, neither should it be too dry so as not to apply easily. Ministers who are making the application should constantly rub their thumb and forefinger in the mixture in order for the elements to reach the correct consistency.

St. Valentine's Day—February 14

While St. Valentine's Day is not an official part of Lent, the day usually falls in the season. It may seem strange that in the midst of a time of mourning and reflecting on the redemption of a lost humanity, a church community would pause to reflect on love, but since a large theme of Easter is love, it seems natural to explore some of its human attributes while contemplating its divine character.

Three different persons named Valentine, all of them martyrs, are mentioned in the early martyrologies under the date of February 14. One is described as a priest at Rome and another as bishop of Interamna (modern Terni); these two both appear to have suffered in the latter part of the third century. Of the third Valentine, who suffered in Africa with a number of companions, nothing further is known.

Some experts state that the day and its customs originate from Valentine, a Roman who was martyred for refusing to give up Christianity. He died on February 14, 269, the same day devoted to the celebration of love. He supposedly left a farewell note for the jailer's daughter, who had become his friend, and signed it "From Your Valentine."

The popular customs associated with Valentine's Day had their origin in a conventional belief that on February 14 the birds began to pair. Thus, in Chaucer's *Parliament of Fowles* we read:

> *For this was sent on Seynt Valentynes day*
> *Whan every foul cometh ther to chese his make.*[2]

For this reason, the day was looked upon as specially consecrated for lovers and as a proper occasion for writing love letters and sending lovers' tokens. Both the French and English literature of the 14th and 15th centuries contain allusions to the practice.

Lent is a season of soul searching and repentance and a time of study and prayer. It is a season for reflection and taking stock. A wise pastor or leader will use this time to help his or her congregation reflect, self-examine, and pray to prepare for the celebration of Easter.

5

HOLY WEEK AND EASTER

∞

Holy Week is the last week of Lent, immediately preceding Easter Sunday, and is a great opportunity for churches to remember the events leading up to Easter. These events challenge us to look behind the joyful celebrations of Palm Sunday and Easter to the suffering, humiliation, and death culminating on Good Friday. Many churches commemorate and reenact the suffering (Passion) and death of Jesus through various observances and services of worship.

Palm Sunday

Palm Sunday is the Sunday before Easter and recalls the triumphal entry of Jesus into Jerusalem on the back of a donkey that had not been ridden. Kings of old entering a city in peace had long followed this tradition. Jesus was met with cheering throngs of worshippers waving palm branches and declaring Him the messianic king. While enacting the prophecy of Zech. 9:9, Jesus showed the humility that characterized His ministry.

Traditionally, worshippers reenact the entry of Jesus into Jerusalem by waving palm branches and singing songs of celebration. Often children process into the church, waving their homemade palm branches and singing joyous songs.

This Sunday is also known as Passion Sunday, since it commemorates the beginning of Holy Week and Jesus' final agonizing journey to the Cross. Webster defines *passion* as "the sufferings of Christ in the period following the Last Supper and including the Crucifixion."[1] The English word *passion* comes from a Latin word *passio*, which means "to suffer," the same word from which we derive the English word *patient*.

Palm Sunday should not only focus on joy but also reflect on what Jesus did on behalf of a fallen humanity. This week is set aside to remember the suffering and death of Jesus as the slain Lamb of God. Uplifting the dual themes of death and resurrection on Palm Sunday points the congregation toward the way of the Cross and better equips them to celebrate His victory on Easter Sunday.

Practical Idea

The ministers distribute large nails to those gathered on Palm Sunday. I usually choose large spikes of different lengths. People are encouraged to carry the nail with them throughout the week as a reminder of what Jesus has done for them. This act also has the potential of witnessing to the grace and love of God in their lives. As people ask why they carry the nails, individuals are able to share their faith and the reason for the season. These nails are brought back to the church for the Good Friday service.

Wednesday of Holy Week

To draw attention to the variety of issues and events surrounding Christ's Passion, Wednesday may be useful as another evening of worship. It might be an appropriate evening to participate in a traditional foot washing service (John 13). This service offers a time for reflection upon the servant nature of what Jesus did as He journeyed to the Cross. It also provides an opportunity for pastors and leaders alike to humbly serve one another.

Foot washing symbolizes a tradition of service. On the evening Jesus was betrayed,

he poured water into a basin and began to wash his disciples' feet, drying them with the towel that was wrapped around him. . . . When he had finished washing their feet, he put on his clothes and returned to his place. "Do you understand what I have done for you?" he asked them. . . . "Now that I, your Lord and Teacher, have washed your feet, you also should wash one another's feet." (John 13:5, 12, 14)

What was Jesus seeking to teach? Jesus said, "I have set you an example that you should do as I have done for you" (v. 15). Jesus performed this act in order to encourage the disciples to live a life of genuine service. When Jesus told them to wash one another's feet, He meant that they should serve one another. The disciples should humble themselves and be willing to do even menial tasks for one another.

During this service pastors and leaders wash the feet of those with whom they serve, such as staff, board members, and elders. The sharing of words of appreciation and affirmation for services rendered can add great meaning to this time of year. Many congregations offer foot washing as part of the Maundy Thursday service. It is suggested that men wash the feet of men and women wash the feet of women.

Maundy (Holy) Thursday

Maundy (Holy) Thursday commemorates the institution of the Lord's Supper (Holy Communion or the Eucharist) and is the oldest of the Holy Week observances. The word *maund* means commandment or new commandment. This evening is set aside to remember Christ's redemptive act, and it is an opportunity to celebrate the last meal that Christ shared with His disciples.

The Last Supper, the agony of Jesus in the Garden of Gethsemane, and Judas's betrayal of Jesus are all remembered on this day. What is called the Last Supper was in fact a celebration of the Passover meal. Jesus gathered with His disciples on the evening of the Passover. As usual the town of Jerusalem was crowded because of the celebration of Passover. The Passover feast was an annual event to commemorate the release of the children of Israel who had been enslaved in Egypt for 400 years. The angel of death "passed over" the houses of the Israelites after they had performed the rite of blood that would provide protection. Each year at the seder supper, as the Passover meal is called, families would recall the 10 plagues and the mighty hand of God that freed them from slavery. To this celebration Jesus placed himself as the Pascal Lamb and His blood as the new wine of forgiveness.

During the meal Judas left to arrange for the betrayal of Jesus. After the meal Jesus and His disciples left the Upper Room and journeyed to the Garden of Gethsemane. In the garden Jesus agonized in prayer as His crucifixion drew nearer. This scene is a vivid picture of the suffering of Jesus, as His human nature struggled with the redemptive plan of God.

Traditionally, churches celebrate Holy Communion on this evening. Some congregations may also include foot washing as described above. A third option is to perform a dramatic presentation of the *Living Last Supper*. Other dramatic presentations would also be appropriate. These would be followed by a celebration of Holy Communion. A fourth option would be to celebrate a traditional Jewish seder meal. Hagadahs,[2] a Jewish worship guide, and other guides are available in a variety of places to explain the seder.

However it is celebrated, the meal on Maundy Thursday is especially tied to the theme of remembering. Jesus and His disciples remembered God's acts of deliverance in their history as they shared the Passover meal together. As we celebrate in our own ways, we gather to remember that Jesus created a new act of deliverance that unfolds throughout the rest of Holy Week.

Good Friday

The Friday of Holy Week has been traditionally called Good Fri-

day. On this day the Church commemorates Jesus' arrest, trial, crucifixion, suffering, death, and burial. Services on Good Friday are designed to direct worshippers to experience some sense of the loneliness, pain, humiliation, and suffering that Christ endured as he
journeyed to the Cross. In some traditions, worship is held at 3 P.M.,
the hour of Jesus' death attested to in Scripture, but other times may
be desirable depending on each congregation's situation. There are
many themes from which a pastor can choose to order the service. A
few are mentioned below.

Focusing on the *seven last words of Christ* as recorded in the
Gospels can provide an outline for the Good Friday service.

"Father, forgive them" (Luke 23:34).

"Today you will be with me in paradise" (Luke 23:43).

"Woman, here is your son" (John 19:26-27).

"My God, my God" (Matt. 27:46; Mark 15:34).

"I am thirsty" (John 19:28).

"It is finished" (John 19:30).

"Father, into your hands" (Luke 23:46).

The *stations of the cross* is yet another format that has proven to
be a significantly reflective time of worship. The stations have a long
history within Catholicism but are becoming more popular among
Protestants. This service uses paintings or banners to represent various scenes from Jesus' betrayal, arrest, trial, and death. Stations may
be set up around a sanctuary or church facility enabling worshippers
to physically move to the various stations. At each of the stations
worshippers could listen to prerecorded music, sing hymns, or pray as
the story is retold. With the advanced technology available in many
churches, worship leaders could digitize all of the pictures of the stations, enabling the people to move through the various stations
without ever leaving the chair or pew.

Another common service for Good Friday is *Tenebrae*, Latin for
"shadows" or "darkness." This term may be applied to all church

services that are part of the last three days of Holy Week. More specifically, however, it has been used in reference to the evening worship on Good Friday. Although many variations of this service appear, it generally contains Scripture readings, hymns, choruses, or special songs. Meditations may be in the form of responsive readings, readers theater, a pastoral homily, or a children's story. The most significant feature of this service is the gradual extinguishing of the lights and candles in the room. The entire service is enacted in stages while the lights are dimmed and/or the candles are gradually extinguished to symbolize the growing darkness not only of Jesus' death but also of hopelessness in the world without God. The service ends in darkness, with a final candle, the Christ candle, carried out of the sanctuary, symbolizing the death of Jesus. Often the service concludes with a loud noise, such as the striking of a large gong, symbolizing the closing of Jesus' tomb. The worshippers leave the service in silence to wait with anticipation for Resurrection Sunday.

Nailing our sins to the cross. This very meaningful service, which became a tradition in the places where I pastored, makes use of an old wooden hewn cross. This cross is carried into the sanctuary and laid on the platform. During the service individuals bring the nails they have carried with them since Palm Sunday and nail them to the cross. This symbolizes the nailing of their burdens and sins upon the cross with Jesus.

Since services on this day are to observe Jesus' death, and since partaking of the Lord's Supper is a celebration, traditionally Holy Communion is not administered on Good Friday. Also, all pictures, statues, and the cross are usually covered in mourning black. The chancel and altar coverings are either removed at the end of the Maundy Thursday service or replaced with black, and altar candles are extinguished. These coverings and symbols of mourning are left this way through Saturday but are always replaced with white before sunrise on Sunday.

Holy Saturday

Holy Saturday was a day of sorrow for the friends of Jesus. The disciples were in a dark and hopeless mood, since Jesus was dead in the tomb. Traditionally, this has been a day of quiet meditation as Christians contemplate the possible fate of a world without a future and without hope apart from God and His grace. This is a time of weeping that lasts for the night (Easter vigil) while awaiting the joy that "comes in the morning" (Ps. 30:5). This is no longer a day of joy, but one of joy and sadness intermingled; it is the close of Lent and penance and the beginning of paschal time, which is one of rejoicing. Often this day was accompanied by a severe fast, which was to abstain from every kind of food.

The Vigil of Easter

The Easter vigil has a long history in the Church. Usually beginning after sundown on the Saturday of Holy Week, this service is a time of prayer and anticipation of the resurrection of Jesus. The vigil can take many forms and last different lengths of time, from an hour of meditative prayer to an entire night of prayer culminating at sunrise. In some traditions those who were preparing during Lent for baptism are baptized at the vigil. Most churches today have placed elements of the vigil in the Easter Sunrise Service.

The Easter vigil begins with darkness. It is the darkness of our world and the darkness of our heart. We begin by preparing ourselves to face the darkness, identifying not only with the mood of the disciples but also with our own sense of sin and darkness. Then a light is struck. It breaks into the darkness. This candle is processed into the space where the community is gathered. When the candle is brought to the front, an Easter proclamation is made. This proclamation can be in the form of a poem or prayer or announcement. It is to be a joyful moment. The idea is to give thanks and praise over this symbol of the Light of Christ in our midst and its representation of Christ's presence among us.

Nine readings and eight psalms form the bulk of the remainder of the service. Each reading is followed by a time of silence, followed by a prayer from a member of the congregation. After the last reading, the candles are lit and the bells ring as the congregation sings a song of glory and praise for the resurrection of Jesus and the victory of our God over sin and death, for us.

Some traditions invite people to be baptized. A time of testimony and celebration surround this part of the evening. The last event of the evening is the sharing of the eucharistic meal. The event is closed with the singing of a joyful hymn and a blessing of praise.

The tomb is empty. There is light in the midst of darkness. The Word has provided spiritual food, and the waters of baptism have given forth new life. The eucharistic meal has been shared, receiving once again the new life that Jesus promises to give to those who believe in Him. And for the first time since Ash Wednesday the congregation sings, shouts, and proclaims—Alleluia, Alleluia.

The Resurrection of Our Lord (Easter Sunday)

"Christ is risen!"

"He is risen, indeed! Alleluia!"

With these words followers of Jesus begin Easter Sunday. Easter, or the Sunday of the resurrection of our Lord, is the day Christians celebrate God raising Christ Jesus from the dead. From its earliest beginning the Church understood His resurrection to be the central witness of God's redeeming act in history by vindicating Jesus as the Messiah and proclaiming Him Lord of all. This event marks the central faith confession of the Early Church and is the focal point for Christian worship. Since the Gospels tell us that Jesus was raised on the first day of the week, His resurrection was observed on the first day of each week.

Even though the Church placed highest emphasis on this event, annual celebrations of the Resurrection did not begin until the fourth century. Since Easter is the most celebrated of the historic seasons of the church year, congregations who celebrate no other Christian festivals usually celebrate Easter. Christ's resurrection is the central pillar on which the Christian faith is built. Good Friday, the day of the Crucifixion, sets the stage for God's ultimate victory on Easter Sunday.

Without the Resurrection, there would be no Christian Church; thus, Easter was the first holiday of the Church.

Popular Customs of the Season

Easter eggs. Eggs have become a common part of Easter. In the United States children look forward to Easter egg hunts where they search for colored eggs, some of which are filled with different goodies. Other countries use brightly colored eggs as symbols of resurrection. Eggs have long been a symbol of life and hope, but it became a particularly apt symbol for Christians. Like a tomb, the baby chick is sealed away from the world. The chick pecks its way out of its tomb to begin life. When Christ rose again from the tomb, He made possible the "new life" of His believers who were entombed in sin.

The story of Simon the Cyrene is a wonderful tale. Romanian custom states that as Simon was returning from the market with a basket of eggs, he was pressed into service by the Roman guards to carry the cross of Jesus (Luke 23:26). When he returned, he found his basket still there, but the eggs inside had been miraculously colored in bright hues.

Russian Orthodox believers have added a different hopeful element to the colored eggs. Before cracking them open and eating them, it is necessary to determine who will receive the good luck from the egg. While one person holds an Easter egg with his or her fingers wrapped around it, leaving only the top portion of the eggshell unprotected, the other person taps his or her egg against it. They exchange taps, egg to egg, until someone's egg cracks. The person whose egg does not crack receives the good luck.

In Romania every worshipper carries wooden eggs. When a person meets another Christian, they declare, "Christ is risen," while extending their brightly colored egg. The other person responds, "He is risen indeed," while tapping his or her egg on the end of the other.

Sunrise services. As the women awoke at dawn that first Easter to perform the rites of preparation to the Lord's body, so Christians for centuries have attended services at dawn on Easter Sunday to praise and pray. Moravians residing in Bethlehem, Pennsylvania, held the first sunrise service in the United States in 1743. This group of new immigrants started the custom in 1732 by going at dawn on Easter to their church's graveyard in Herrnhut, Saxony (now Germany), for worship and praise to imitate the women that first Easter morning. The minister would mount the podium and loudly address the congregation with "The Lord is risen." The congregation responded, "The Lord is risen, indeed," then they would sing joyful hymns until the sun fully appeared, whereupon they walked to their God's Acre cemetery and reaffirmed their belief in a resurrected Lord.

Easter lilies. Many congregations bring in lilies to adorn the sanctuary. "These beautiful trumpet-shaped white flowers symbolize purity, innocence, hope and life—the spiritual essence of Easter."[3] Often people purchase lilies in memory of a loved one, a friend, or someone they wish to honor. When using them it is a good idea to remove the yellow stamen because of the pollen.

White paraments and vestments. White is the color of Easter, so sanctuaries are often decorated with white paraments on the altar, clerical vestments are white, and a white cloth is placed upon the cross.

Ringing of bells. As is common at Christmas, the ringing of bells to celebrate the Resurrection is an important event in the worship of many congregations. Often children ring these bells, marching through the congregation and singing. Sometimes bell choirs perform or cathedral bells are rung. The idea is to usher in a spirit of joy.

The Sundays After Easter

Holy Humor Sunday

Many churches are resurrecting an old Easter custom begun by the Greeks in the early centuries of Christianity. Holy Humor Sunday, or Bright Sunday, is the Sunday after Easter. It is to be observed as a day of joy and laughter in celebration of the resurrection of Jesus. Some carry the theme of "the joke is on you, Satan." The custom is rooted in the musings of Early Church theologians (such as Augustine, Gregory of Nyssa, and John Chrysostom). They claimed that God played a practical joke on the devil by raising Jesus from the dead. The early theologians called it *Risus paschalis*—"the Easter laugh." Churchgoers and pastors played practical jokes on one another, told jokes, sang silly songs, and danced.

One only needs to search the Internet to find how widespread Holy Humor Sunday has become. Many of the liturgies on the Internet are filled with jokes and bright, happy songs. One of my friends, a Presbyterian pastor, has observed Holy Humor Sunday for years. One of his present lay associates visited the church for the first time on that Sunday and has come ever since.

Ideas: The children could do a comedic skit where Satan is vanquished, laughed at, and so on. Someone can write a fractured poem much like "The Night Before Christmas" but focusing on the victory of Jesus over the plans of Satan. There are many more ideas on the Internet.[4]

Ascension Day (or Sunday)

Ascension Day commemorates the ascension of Jesus into heaven following His crucifixion and resurrection (Acts 1:6-11). During the 40-day period after His resurrection, Jesus preached and intermingled with His apostles and disciples. Ascension Day marks not only the resurrection of Jesus from the dead but also His exaltation to Ruler and Lord.

The first readers of Acts, no doubt, believed that Jesus ascended to a literal heaven and would return from God's throne "someplace up there" at the end of time. The point of the story is found in the angelic challenge, "Why do you stand here looking into the sky?" (Acts 1:11). The idea of this passage is that we have work to do in this lifetime, this present world. This world is not the front porch to eternity, nor is it worthless in light of eternity. Rather, our life is in the here and now. Heaven is heaven and earth is earth, and both are beautiful! Our calling as Christians is to heal and transform the world—*this* world. It has been said that there are some people who are "so heavenly minded that they are of no earthly good." The temptation for the disciples, as it is for us, is to gaze at the heavens, to wait for a Second Coming, and to forget that our calling is to live faithfully in this life as God's partners in healing the world.

Eternal life is not "the pie in the sky when you die in the sweet by and by," but companionship and awareness of God in the present moment. This moment is a holy moment and this day, a beautiful day. As the psalmist says, "This is the day the LORD has made; let us rejoice and be glad in it" (Ps. 118:24). Our pastoral task in preaching is to help persons experience eternity in the midst of time.

Celebrating the Ascension gives us a forum to talk about our mission to participate in the kingdom of God, between the time that Jesus left and is coming again.

Ideas: Early in the history of the Church, on the night before Ascension Sunday, church leaders would gather for a vigil. In some traditions this is when the paschal candle, which was lit on Easter Sunday, is extinguished. This can also be a part of the service on Sunday. The emphasis is upon the finished work of Jesus and the celebration of His ascending with the promise of returning.

Some churches use drama to communicate something special on this day, either by the raising of a statue or someone actually ascending.

This is also a great day for a church potluck celebration with readings about Christ's ascension.

Mother's Day

While Mother's Day is not a part of the church calendar, it is a holiday that many churches remember as an opportunity to remind mothers worldwide of how important they are.

In the United States Mother's Day is celebrated on the second Sunday in May. In 17th-century England an annual observance called Mothering Sunday was celebrated on the fourth Sunday of Lent. On Mothering Sunday the servants, who generally lived with their employers, were encouraged to return home and honor their mothers. President Wilson made Mother's Day an official holiday in 1914.

Pentecost Sunday

Pentecost is originally a Jewish festival, which begins on the 50th day after the beginning of Passover; in the Christian calendar it falls on the seventh Sunday after Easter. Pentecost was called the Feast of Weeks (*Shavuot*), and in the Old Testament was originally an agricultural festival celebrating and giving thanks for the "first fruits" of the early spring harvest (Lev. 23; Exod. 23, 34).

By the early New Testament period this festival had gradually lost its association with agriculture and became associated with the celebration of God's creation and religious history. With the destruction of Jerusalem in A.D. 70, the festival began to focus exclusively on God's gracious gift of Torah (the "Law") on Mount Sinai. It continues to be celebrated in this manner in modern Judaism.

While other references to Pentecost occur in the New Testament (such as 1 Cor. 16:8), it is most significant in Acts 2 with the familiar scene of the outpouring of the Holy Spirit on those in the Upper Room. Luke associates the events of Acts 2 with Pentecost, and Peter relates it in his sermon to the prophecies of Joel 2 and the promises of Jesus (Acts 1:8). In both the emphasis is on empowerment through the Holy Spirit to enable the people of God to witness to Jesus the Christ.

Pentecost represents God's gracious, enabling presence actively working among His people, calling and enabling them to live out in dynamic ways the witness of being His people. With this theme the Pentecost celebrations of Christianity and Judaism are similar, since in Judaism the Torah, God's instruction to His people, is the means by which they become God's witnesses to the world.

For Christians Pentecost Sunday is a day to celebrate the hope evoked by knowing that God through the Holy Spirit is at work among His people. It is a celebration of newness, re-creation, and renewal of purpose, mission, and God's ongoing work in the world. Yet, it is also a recognition that God's work is done through His people as He pours out His presence on them.

This focus on the Church's mission to the world and the empowering presence of God through the Holy Spirit in the Church should provide a powerful impetus for churches, especially those in the evangelical traditions, to recover this season of the church year. Tremendous opportunities to use this sacred time abound to call people to renewal though the work of the Holy Spirit in their lives.

Ideas: Sermons, drama, and video presentations can enhance the emphasis. This is also a wonderful Sunday to have a guest missionary or to present a mission film. The focus is on the Holy Spirit's movement upon the Church enabling her to move into the world.

If one wanted to deviate from the lectionary, a possible sermon outline could be taken from Acts 1:8. The title could be "Fitness to Witness" and a typical sermon might have these points: "Witness to Family," "Witness to Friends," "Witness to Foes," "Witness to Foreigners." A more postmodern sermon might tell the story of Philip and the Ethiopian ruler and emphasize the filling of the Holy Spirit to enable Philip to minister so boldly. There are many ways to go on this incredibly exciting Sunday.

THE CHURCH CYCLE

Go and make disciples

of all nations, baptizing them

in the name of the Father and of

the Son and of the Holy Spirit,

and teaching them to obey everything

I have commanded you.

And surely I am with you always,

to the very end of the age.

—Matt. 28:19-20

6

ORDINARY TIME

∞

If the faithful are to mature in their spiritual lives and increase in faith, they must descend the great mountain peaks of Easter and Christmas in order to "pasture" in the vast verdant meadows of *tempus annum*, or Ordinary Time. As the Church journeys through time, the reference to Christ's resurrection and the weekly recurrence of this redemptive act are reminders of the "pilgrim nature and eschatological character of the People of God."[1]

Ordinary Time is the longest portion of the church year. It fills the weeks that do not celebrate a specific aspect of the mystery of Christ. The Christmas cycle honors the birth of Christ, and the Easter cycle rejoices in the Resurrection. Ordinary Time is devoted to the mystery of Christ in all His aspects, especially those dealing with the whole Church.

The term *Ordinary Time* may be misleading. In the context of the liturgical year the term *ordinary* does not mean "usual or average" but rather "not seasonal." This term comes from the word *ordinal*, which simply means counted time. Ordinary Time is that part of the liturgical year that lies outside the seasons of Christmas (and Advent) and Easter (and Lent). The Sundays between the baptism of our Lord (the first Sunday after Epiphany) and Transfiguration Sunday (the Sunday before Ash Wednesday) is in some traditions also part of Ordinary Time. The readings during worship in Ordinary Time help to instruct us on how to live out our Christian faith in our daily lives.

Counted time after Pentecost always begins with Trinity Sunday (the first Sunday after Pentecost) and ends with Christ the King Sunday or the Reign of Christ the King (the last Sunday after Pentecost or last Sunday of the church year). The number of weeks after Pentecost is counted backward from Christ the King.

Trinity Sunday

The first Sunday after Pentecost is the Festival of the Holy Trinity or Trinity Sunday. On this day the Church honors and marvels in the mystery of God's triune nature: Father, Son, and Holy Spirit (three-in-one and one-in-three). How God can be one God in three distinct persons stretches human understanding; thus, Christians accept this doctrine as a mystery.

The issues surrounding the doctrine of the Trinity cannot be solved here, but the point that can be made is this: our congregations are starving, not for doctrinal correctness, but for life in communion with the triune God. Our churches need the subversive presence of the triune God who is active and at work in our lives. The whole people of God are yearning to be encountered by the God who gives up the idea of God (Phil. 2:5-11) and becomes incarnate in the demands and struggles of daily life. We long for this incarnate God. Baptized into this faith, we are born to proclaim before the world, the God who by the power of the Spirit animates Christian worship in the name of Jesus Christ.

Trinity Sunday was instituted to provide opportunity to worship and talk about the most holy Trinity. Even though there were early controversies and heresies surrounding the doctrine of the Trinity, it has become a fundamental article of faith.

Andrei Rublev painted an amazing picture to express how he understood the concept of the Trinity. It depicts three persons seated around a round table. Each of them has the same face but is wearing different garments. There is controversy whether this image depicts the three angels who visited Abraham at the Oak of Mamre, or whether it is his understanding of Holy Trinity.

The theological concept of *perichoresis*, which means "the divine dance," is a Greek term used to describe the triune relationship between each person of the Godhead. The idea is that they are equal but separate. It can be defined as co-indwelling, co-inhering, and mutual interpenetration. Alister McGrath writes that the term *perichoresis*

> allows the individuality of the persons to be maintained, while insisting that each person shares in the life of the other two. An image often used to express this idea is that of a "community of being," in which each person, while maintaining its distinctive identity, penetrates the others and is penetrated by them.[2]

The Trinity is an example of love on a divine scale. It is a model to humans and an example of how they are to love one another. Trinity Sunday provides an opportunity for pastors to educate and encourage their congregations through a variety of presentations: sermons, debates, drama, videos, and so on. Many congregants in Western churches know little about this doctrine and its importance. Pastors should not overlook this Sunday as a discipling and teaching opportunity.

Father's Day

Father's Day, like Mother's Day, is not a part of the church year, but it is a great opportunity for the Church to celebrate with fathers of all ages and honor them for their role. President Coolidge supported the idea of a national Father's Day in 1924, and in 1966 President Johnson declared that the third Sunday in June is to be observed as Father's Day.

Reformation Sunday

The Church celebrates Reformation Sunday on the last Sunday of October, commemorating a significant event in the history of the Reformed tradition. The Protestant Reformation resulted from Martin Luther's disenchantment with the Roman Catholic Church. Martin Luther was a Catholic monk, priest, and theology professor in Germany who was bothered by certain practices, including the sale of indulgences, whereby people appeared to be able to buy their way to forgiveness. Luther started to write a complaint, which became a list of 95 abuses in the Roman church. On October 31, 1517, he nailed a copy of his "95 Theses" to the church door in Wittenberg, Germany.

The Roman church asked him to withdraw his objections, and when he would not, he was excommunicated from the church. Germans, anxious to sever Roman ties, widely accepted Luther's ideas, thus propelling him to lead the movement in Western Europe.

Pastors can use themes, ideas, and historical references to make this a meaningful discussion of what makes one a "Protestant," by showing the common theological thread that weaves its way through the tradition. Remembering the Reformation is a way for pastors to show that churches have more in common than the differences that easily divide the kingdom of God.

All Hallows Eve (October 31)

For many people Halloween has become synonymous with candy, costumes, witches, ghosts, and pumpkins. The true origins of Halloween lie within the ancient Celtic tribes who lived in Ireland, Scotland, Wales, and Brittany. For the Celts November 1 marked the beginning of a new year and the coming of winter. The night before the new year, they celebrated the festival of Samhain, which means summer's end. It is a time to celebrate the harvest and think about everything going into a dark silence. During this festival the Celts believed that the souls of the dead, including ghosts, goblins, and witches, returned to mingle with the living. In order to scare away the evil spirits, people would wear masks and light bonfires. When the Romans conquered the Celts, they added their own touches to the Samhain festival, including making centerpieces out of apples and nuts for Pomona, the Roman goddess of the orchards. The Romans also bobbed for apples and drank cider, traditions that are still practiced on this date.

In 835 Pope Gregory IV moved the commemoration for all the martyrs (later, all saints) from May 13 to November 1. The night before this commemoration became known as All Hallows Eve or "holy evening." Eventually, the name was shortened to Halloween.

The purpose of this feast is to remember the saints who have died, both canonized saints and the saints that make up the Body of Christ (using Paul's definition in his Epistles). It is a celebration of the "communion of saints," which reminds us that the Church is not bound by space or time. The writer of the Epistle to the Hebrews says, "Therefore, since we are surrounded by such a great cloud of witnesses, let us throw off everything that hinders and the sin that so easily entangles, and let us run with perseverance the race marked out for us" (12:1). Those "saints" who have gone on before and those "saints" that walk among us remind us that we are part of something that is bigger than us.

All Hallows Eve, the evening before All Saints' Day, became an evening the Church set aside for prayer, contemplation, worship, and dedication to God. Halloween is an opportunity for the people of God, in the midst of the celebration of harvest and harmless fun, to again remember and rejoice in those who advanced the faith of the Great King by the giving of their lives.

Practical Ideas for Halloween

Halloween is dominated by consumerism in modern society, and yet the Church can still find much that is worthy of redeeming. Teaching children the history of the Church and the sacrifices people have made for the preservation and propagation of the faith is essential. Many churches today have "alternative" parties, but these parties should not simply be in opposition to Halloween but rather should be opportunities for children to have fun and learn about their faith. For example, you could have children dress up in costumes that reflect a spiritual or historic character. They could dress as a biblical character or a preacher or some famous Christian. Activities could reflect a spiritual tone or teaching.

All Saints' Day—November 1

All Saints' Day is a universal festival that honors and remembers all Christian saints, known and unknown. The Western church commemorates the saints on November 1. The Orthodox churches observe it on the first Sunday after Pentecost.

Roman Catholics, the Orthodox, Anglicans, and Lutherans celebrate All Saints' Day, but because of their differing understandings of the identity and function of the saints, the rituals in these churches widely differ. For Roman Catholics, the Orthodox, and some Anglicans, All Saints' is a day to remember, give thanks for, and also venerate and pray to the saints in heaven for intercession. The day is observed by Lutherans through remembering and thanking God for all saints, both dead and living. It is a day to glorify Jesus Christ, who by His holy life and death has made the saints holy through baptism and faith.

Although many Protestant churches, such as the Lutherans and Episcopalians, continued to observe All Saints' Day after the Reformation, many others did not. Today evangelical groups in the United States often overlook it. This omission is unfortunate, since All Saints' Day is a good reminder of the faith that built the Church.

Christ the King Sunday

Christ the King is the last Sunday after Pentecost, thus the last Sunday of the church year. This day completes the annual journey through the life of Jesus Christ that began by preparing for His birth during Advent.

On this Sunday Christians are reminded that Jesus came as the Great King. Kings are absolute rulers; they attain power by raising and leading armies into war against other countries. Jesus' war was not against people or against a country, but rather against sin, death, and the power of the devil. By His death, resurrection, and ascension, Jesus won the war against evil.

All Christians are asked to do is to know that Jesus fought and won the war for their sakes and to recognize Him as King of Kings. On Christ the King Sunday Christians recognize and worship Christ as King of heaven and earth for all time without challenge and without end.

Thanksgiving Day

The national holiday of Thanksgiving occurs every fourth Thursday in November in the United States. Thanksgiving is a wonderful day to pause and give thanks for God's generosity and provision for another year. The president of the United States makes a proclamation, governors of the 50 states add their own messages, and Americans gather as families to feast and be thankful for what God has done in their lives the past year. A day of thanksgiving is a custom that most cultures have and that the forefathers of the United States brought with them to the new world.

The celebration in 1621, initiated at Plymouth, is often considered the first Thanksgiving of the New World. The pilgrims were merely carrying on a tradition from their former lands, a tradition of thanking God for a bounteous harvest. The voyagers on the Mayflower had expected to land somewhere near the Jamestown colony in a relatively benign climate, but they were ill-prepared for the harsh winter that followed and nearly half their number died. They persevered by planting crops with the help of a wonderful native Squanto. They built wooden houses and in October were blessed with a rich harvest.

In 1622, nothing seemed to have sparked a celebration, but in 1623 after a sudden rain saved the crop, they decided to celebrate the harvest again, this time in November. Bradford ordered "all the Pilgrims with your wives and little ones, to gather at the meeting house, on the hill . . . there to listen to the pastor, and render thanksgiving to the Almighty God for all His blessings." Although the early settlers did not always celebrate Thanksgiving, they did it often enough until it become a custom.

After being elected president, George Washington proclaimed Thursday, November 26, 1789, a day of national thanksgiving. He also requested that citizens assemble in churches that day to thank God for His goodness toward them. Washington repeated the act in 1795, but his fellow citizens did not catch the spirit, and the holiday was not repeated nationally for some time. Sarah Josepha Hale, a New Englander and editor of the *American Ladies Magazine* in Boston, wrote an annual editorial supporting a national holiday of giving thanks. Finally, in 1863, in the midst of the Civil War, she wrote an editorial that struck a nerve:

> Would it not be a great advantage, socially, nationally, religiously, to have the day of our American Thanksgiving positively settled? Putting aside the sectional feelings, and local incidents that might be urged by any single State or isolated territory that desired to choose its own time would it not be more noble, more truly American, to become national in unity when we offer to God our tribute of joy and gratitude for the blessings of the year?[3]

In July 1863, 170,000 Americans had squared off against one another in the titanic Battle of Gettysburg, which produced the first real defeat of the Southern Army of Virginia under Robert E. Lee. It also produced staggering casualties. President Lincoln was looking for a way not only to be thankful for the victory but also to bind the wounds of a shattered nation. On October 3, 1863, he issued a proclamation setting aside the last Thursday in November 1863 as a national Thanksgiving Day in order to not forget that prosperity and freedom were God's gifts:

> It has seemed to me fit and proper that they should be solemnly, reverently and gratefully acknowledged as with one heart and one voice by the whole American people. I do, therefore, invite my fellow citizens in every part of the United States, and also those who are at sea and those who are sojourning in foreign lands, to set part and observe the last Thursday of November next as a day of thanksgiving and praise to our beneficent Father who dwelleth in the heavens.[4]

Often Thanksgiving Sunday falls on the first Sunday of Advent. While mention of this wonderful celebration is appropriate, it must not take away from Advent.

Ideas: Pastors could use a variety of prayers and hymns or songs to emphasize the idea of gratitude. The Great Thanksgiving Prayer in the *Book of Common Prayer* is a wonderful way to bring in a eucharistic theme to the celebration of Thanksgiving. Liturgies for Thanksgiving Day celebrations can be found on the Internet.

Conclusion

There is nothing of so much consequence as a reasoned and celebrated understanding of practical religion. The church year provides an opportunity for a pastor and congregation not only to celebrate numerous special days but also to understand the history and theology of the Christian faith. As a way for pastors and leaders of congregations to teach the rudimentary tenets of the Christian faith, the church year is truly a resource for all seasons.

APPENDIXES

APPENDIX 1

Advent and Christmas

Ideas for Public Presentation of Advent

(The following worship presentations are merely suggestions. They are designed to introduce each of the weeks of Advent. You are welcome to use them in their entirety or to create your own presentations.

Each week has a key word that reflects one of the themes of Advent. Since Advent is a time of preparation for the coming of the Lord Jesus, both as the Babe of Bethlehem and the coming Victorious King, the key words—*hope, peace, joy,* and *love*—reflect four main ideas from Jesus' ministry. Advent celebrations differ from community to community, with different key words sometimes assigned to different weeks. For example, some of these words differ from the key words that are in the "Advent Family Worship Guide" in Appendix 2. What is important is to have a candlelighting ceremony of some sort to educate your congregation in the motifs of the season.)

THE CANDLES OF ADVENT
THE FIRST SUNDAY OF ADVENT: PROPHECY
THE CANDLE OF HOPE

(The presenters are encouraged to pick a scripture appropriate for this Sunday. A number of readers can be used.)

READER: Today is the first Sunday of Advent. *Advent* means "coming," and in this season we prepare for the coming of Christ. One of the ways we prepare for His coming is by making an Advent wreath and lighting its candles to remind us of the gifts Christ brings to the world.

READER: The Advent wreath includes many symbols to help us think about Christ and His gifts. The wreath itself is in the shape of a circle. A circle has no beginning and no end. This reminds us that there is no beginning and no end to God and that God's love and caring are forever.

READER: The light from the candles—that grows stronger each Sunday in Advent—reminds us that Jesus is the Light of the World.

READER: Today we light the candle of hope. The people of Israel hoped in God's promises and were not disappointed. Again and again God delivered Israel from its enemies. We, too, have the same experience of salvation. That is why we believe in God's promise to send Jesus to us once again to judge the world and establish His kingdom forever upon the earth. *(A person lights the candle.)*

READER: Hope is like a light shining in a dark place. As we look at the light of this candle, we celebrate the hope we have in Jesus Christ.

READER *(Read Scripture)*

READER: Let us pray: "Thank You, God, for the hope You give us. We ask that as we wait for all Your promises to come true, and for Christ to come again, that You would remain present with us. Help us today and every day to worship You, to hear Your word, and to do Your will by sharing Your hope with each other. We ask it in the name of the One who was born in Bethlehem. Amen."

(Participants return to their seats.)

THE SECOND SUNDAY OF ADVENT: BETHLEHEM
THE CANDLE OF PEACE

(The presenters are encouraged to pick a scripture appropriate for this Sunday.)

READER: Last Sunday we lit the first candle in our Advent wreath, the prophecy candle, which is the candle of hope. We light it again as we remember that Christ, who was born in Bethlehem, will come again to fulfill all of God's promises to us. *(A person lights the candle of hope.)*

READER: The second candle of Advent is the candle of peace, representing Bethlehem, the birthplace of our Jesus. *Peace* is a word that we hear a lot. It is one of the things that we hope for. Christ brought peace when He first came to us, and He will bring everlasting peace when He comes again.

READER: The prophet Isaiah called Christ "the Prince of Peace." When Jesus came, He taught people the importance of being peacemakers. He said that those who make peace shall be called the children of God.

READER: We light the candle of peace to remind us that Jesus is the Prince of Peace and that through Him peace is found. *(A person lights the candle of peace.)*

READER: Peace is like a light shining in a dark place. As we look at this candle, we celebrate the peace we find in Jesus Christ.

READER: Let us pray: "Thank You, God, for the peace You give us. We ask that as we wait for all Your promises to come true, and for Christ to come again, that You would remain present with us. Help us today and every day to worship You, to hear Your word, and to do Your will by sharing Your peace with each other. We ask it in the name of the One who was born in Bethlehem. Amen."

(Participants return to their seats.)

THE THIRD SUNDAY OF ADVENT: SHEPHERD
THE CANDLE OF JOY

(The presenters are encouraged to pick a scripture appropriate for this Sunday.)

READER: The first Sunday of Advent we lit the prophecy candle in our Advent wreath. It is also called the candle of hope. We light it again today as we remember Jesus, who was born Christ and King. And we remember that He will come again to fulfill all of God's promises to us. *(A person lights the candle of hope.)*

READER: Last Sunday we lit the Bethlehem candle, the candle of peace. We light it again today as we remember that Christ, who was born in Bethlehem, has come as Savior and Redeemer. The Babe of Bethlehem has come to bring everlasting peace. *(A person lights the candle of peace.)*

READER: Today we light the third candle of Advent; it is the shepherd candle, the candle of joy. When the angel Gabriel told Mary that a special child would be born to her, Mary was filled with joy. She sang a song that began with the words: "My soul magnifies the Lord, and my spirit has rejoiced in God my Savior" (Luke 1:46-47, NKJV).

READER: Just as the birth of Jesus gave great joy to His mother, so His presence in the world gave joy to those who had none before. He healed them and gave them hope and peace when they believed in Him. From hope, peace, and love grows joy.

READER: Shepherds on the hillside outside the city were told by a multitude of angels that the Babe born in Bethlehem would bring "Joy to the World" but more importantly He would be the "Joy of the World."

READER: We light the candle of joy to remind us that when Jesus is born in us, we have joy and that through Him there will be everlasting joy on earth. (*A person lights the candle of joy.*)

READER: Joy is like a light shining in a dark place. As we look at this candle, we celebrate the joy we find in Jesus Christ.

READER: Let us pray: "Thank You, God, for the joy You give us. We ask that as we wait for all Your promises to come true, and for Christ to come again, that You would remain present with us. Help us today and every day to worship You, to hear Your word, and to do Your will by sharing Your joy with each other. We ask it in the name of the One who was born in Bethlehem. Amen.

(*Participants return to their seats*)

THE FOURTH SUNDAY OF ADVENT: ANGEL
THE CANDLE OF LOVE

(*The presenters are encouraged to pick a scripture appropriate for this Sunday.*)

READER: The first Sunday of Advent we lit the prophecy candle in our Advent wreath; it is also called the candle of hope. We light it again today as we remember Jesus, who was born Christ and King. And we remember that He will come again to fulfill all of God's promises to us. (*A person lights the candle of hope.*)

READER: The second Sunday of Advent we lit the Bethlehem candle, the candle of peace. We light it again today as we remember that Christ, who was born in Bethlehem, has come as Savior and Redeemer. The Babe of Bethlehem has come to bring everlasting peace. (*A person lights the candle of peace.*)

READER: Last Sunday we lit the third candle of Advent; it is the shepherd candle, the candle of joy. When the angel Gabriel told

Mary that a special child would be born to her, she was filled with joy. She sang a song that began with the words: "My soul magnifies the Lord, and my spirit has rejoiced in God my Savior" (Luke 1:46-47, NKJV). (*A person lights the candle of joy.*)

READER: The fourth candle of Advent, the angel candle, is the candle of love. God's love is a perfect love. He holds nothing back. God, in love, gives us everything we need to live a life of hope and peace.

READER: The Bible says, "God so loved the world that He gave His only begotten Son, that whoever believes in Him should not perish but have everlasting life" (John 3:16, NKJV). God comes in Jesus to show us His perfect love.

READER: "Love is kind and patient, never jealous, boastful, proud, or rude. Love isn't selfish or quick tempered. It doesn't keep a record of wrongs that others do. Love rejoices in the truth, but not in evil. Love is always supportive, loyal, hopeful, and trusting" (1 Cor. 13:4-7, CEV).

READER: Love never ends. We light the candle of love to remind us that Jesus brings us God's love and shows us how to love others. (*A person lights the candle of love.*)

READER: Love is like a light shining in a dark place. As we look at this candle we celebrate the love we find in Jesus Christ.

READER: Let us pray: "Thank You, God, for the love You give us. We ask that as we wait for all Your promises to come true, and for Christ to come again, that You would remain present with us. Help us today and every day to worship You, to hear Your word, and to do Your will by sharing Your love with each other. We ask it in the name of the One who was born in Bethlehem. Amen."

(*Participants return to their seats.*)

APPENDIX 2

Advent Family Worship Guide

(Note: The following is an Advent family worship guide. It is designed to be used nightly as a family devotional. Pastors, you are free to make copies and print them for your church families. I recommend that you put this in booklet form.*)

Welcome to Advent. This is a most joyous and wonderful time of the year. I have prepared these study guides to help you find deeper meaning in the Advent celebration.

There is great mystery in the fact that God would care enough about us to enter very personally into our lives. Advent reminds us of this great love.

My prayer for you and your family is that this Christmas season will be more than just a time for food, fellowship, presents, and fun. I pray that it will spark anew in your hearts a deep desire to get closer to the One that made our happiness and joy possible.

Have a joyous and happy Christmastime. Use these guides to enrich your family time. If you will make this nightly ritual a priority, it can become a tradition that will be one of the most meaningful things you do at Christmastime.

From my family to yours, we wish you a very Merry Christmas.

Enthusiastically,
Gary Waller

(Pastors, feel free to exclude this introduction and insert your own. Personalize it for your congregation. However, you are welcome to insert mine as well.)

---

*A printable copy of this worship guide is available online at www.beaconhill books.com/go/thechurchyear.

Advent—What Is It?

The word *Advent* is from the Latin word *adventus,* which means "coming" and refers to the coming of Jesus into our world. Advent comprises the four Sundays preceding Christmas.

For the Early Church, Easter was the major Christian festival. Advent did not become part of the church calendar until the festival of Christmas was established. This came about in the fourth century.

The celebration of the Incarnation—God becoming man—was not very old when the church felt the need for a period of preparation for Christmas celebration.

Advent was originally 40 days long. It represented the 4,000 years of patient waiting on the part of the Hebrews for the promised Messiah.

The Advent Mood

The mood of Advent is best expressed as one of longing for deliverance from oppression, coupled with anticipation of the Messiah.

It is not a season of fasting; it is a season of prayer. The concept of King is uppermost. Jesus is the King of grace.

The Symbols of the Advent Wreath

The purpose of the wreath is to deepen our understanding of Christmas.

1. The base of the wreath is covered with green—the color green testifies to the continuation of life in Christ.

2. The circular base represents life without end—eternal life.

3. The candles signify God's Son as the Light of the World. There are five candles in all. The first, second, and fourth candles are violet to symbolize our penitence and preparation. The third candle is pink to symbolize joy. In the center of the wreath is the white candle, which represents Christ.

HOW TO MAKE AN ADVENT WREATH

The wreath should be in the form of a circle. The base of the wreath can be made from Styrofoam, wire, or wood. Anchor the candleholders securely in the base.

Cover the base with greenery. If live evergreens are used, make sure to protect them from fire. Spraying them with fire retardant is an excellent precaution and will ease your mind.

The wreath has five candles. Four candles are placed on the outside of the circle and one in the middle. Usually three violet candles, one pink candle, and one white candle are used. If you wish, you may use all red or all white candles.

WHAT TO DO EACH DAY

The Advent season will be most meaningful to you if you set aside a special time each day for lighting the Advent candles. Be sure and name each candle as you light it. This would be a great time to read the Scripture and talk about the significance of the holiday season. I have prepared devotionals for each day. Remember the focus of Advent is prayer, so pray together as a family. Make it a practice to include everyone in the celebration.

THE PROPHECY CANDLE

The First Sunday of Advent
Key Word: PREPARE

Christians, take comfort and be glad, for once again the Long-Awaited One stands at our door! Let us prepare our hearts and homes to greet our Lord, Emmanuel.

The first candle is violet. It reminds us of the prophets who expected and predicted the coming of the Messiah who would bring peace and love and salvation to the world.

Jesus said, "I am the light of the world. Whoever follows me will not walk in darkness, but will have the light of life" (John 8:12, ESV).*

O Come, O Come, Emmanuel†

O come, O come, Emmanuel,
And ransom captive Israel,
That mourns in lonely exile here
Until the Son of God appear.

O come, Thou Wisdom from on high,
And order all things far and nigh;
To us the path of knowledge show,
And cause us in her ways to go.

O come, Desire of Nations; bind
All peoples in one heart and mind.
Bid envy, strife, and quarrels cease;
Fill the whole world with heaven's peace.

---

*Scripture quotations marked ESV are from *The Holy Bible, English Standard Version*® (ESV), copyright © 2001 by Crossway Bibles, a publishing ministry of Good News Publishers. Used by permission. All rights reserved.

†Words by unknown author, Latin, 12th century; stanzas 1 and 4 translated by John M. Neale (1818-66); stanzas 2 and 3 translated by Henry S. Coffin (1877—1954).

O come, Thou Dayspring, come and cheer
Our spirits by Thine advent here;
Disperse the gloomy clouds of night,
And death's dark shadows put to flight.

Refrain:
Rejoice! Rejoice! Emmanuel
Shall come to thee, O Israel!

SUNDAY—Isa. 9:2, 6-7

Approximately 750 years before the birth of Christ, God gave the prophet Isaiah these promises about the coming Messiah. The people of Israel were living in darkness. They had a hope that the Messiah would come and bring light to their miserable existence. Jesus did that—He became the Light of the World. Never again will people need to live in darkness and despair. Around our present world we see evidence of people living in darkness and hopelessness. We have the light. During this holiday season how can God use you to help spread His light to a world that cannot see through their darkness, worry, fear, and despair? Discuss the importance of the names for the Messiah in verse 6. Why is this a comfort?

MONDAY—Isa. 61:1

Throughout His life and ministry, Jesus fulfilled the words of this wonderful prophecy: God's Spirit was on Him; He preached good tidings, healed the brokenhearted, proclaimed liberty to the captive, and opened the prison of those that were bound. Today we are fortunate because Jesus continues to perform these messianic roles in our lives.

He preaches good tidings—He is drawing us to himself.

He binds up the broken in heart—many of us who suffer from fractures of the heart have found this promise true.

He proclaims liberty for those who are captive—through Him we can experience freedom from those addictions and sins that control us.

Isaiah reminds us of what Jesus is doing for us if we let Him—He has come to set us free. Paul also voices his response: "It is for freedom that Christ has set us free. Stand firm, then, and do not let yourselves be burdened again by a yoke of slavery" (Gal. 5:1).*

What changes does Jesus want to bring about in you? What do you need for God to do for you today? Ask Him.

TUESDAY—Isa. 40:1-8

What a glorious passage! This passage refers to the coming of a King. In biblical times, before a king would come, everyone would prepare for him. Everything was cleaned, refurbished, painted, and so on, and even crooked roads were straightened and fixed.

The theme of this week has been "prepare." In the midst of the huff and puff of Christmas we need to stop long enough to open our hearts to Jesus. We should not give Him the leftovers but should focus our attention upon His coming. What a tragedy if we spend, spend, spend and find that it was all for nothing; that we were in such a frenzy that we missed the real point and the great joy and contentment of Christmas.

What are you doing to prepare for Jesus' coming? Do others see the preparation in your life?

WEDNESDAY—Isa. 7:14; Matt. 1:23

When this message of Isaiah's was given to Joseph, he was living in Nazareth. Nazareth was not the type of town you would expect a king to call home. In John 1:46, Nathaniel asks, "Nazareth! Can anything good come from there?" "'Come and see,' said Philip." Nazareth, to Nathaniel, was just another drab, quiet, little, country town. But unexpectedly, out of Nazareth came the greatest good the

---

*All Scripture quotations not otherwise designated are from the *Holy Bible, New International Version*® (NIV®). Copyright © 1973, 1978, 1984 by International Bible Society. Used by permission of Zondervan Publishing House. All rights reserved.

world has ever known. *Nazareth* is therefore a word suggesting God's grace. In a humble home in that town, God found a virgin through whom, by His Spirit, the divine Savior would be conceived. There this child would grow up, secure His education, learn a trade, declare His mission, and go forth.

All those who receive Him become His disciples—people of grace. Are you a disciple? If not, it is not too late to begin.

THURSDAY—Matt. 1:1-17

This genealogy in Matthew is the genealogy of a King. There is something symbolic of the whole of human life by the way Jesus' pedigree is arranged. The first section takes the story of history up to David—greatness. The second section takes the story to the exile in Babylon—captivity, shame, tragedy, and disaster. The third section takes the story up to Jesus—liberation from captivity.

These verses also can symbolize three stages in our spiritual histories. Section one tells us that we were born in greatness. We were created in God's image. God's dream for us was for greatness. Section two speaks about how humanity used its free will to defy and disobey God. Section three tells us that greatness can be regained. God did not abandon us but sent His Son to redeem and rescue a lost world.

Praise the Lord for His grace. Center your prayer time as a praise time. Review again God's provision for salvation.

FRIDAY—Luke 1:46-56

Here we have a passage that has become one of the great hymns of the Church—the Magnificat. The key words are *favor* and *grace*. Favor is found in the choice of Mary to bear the most precious of all heavenly gifts. The message from Mary was one of awe and humility. She never felt worthy, yet knew that the honor was a great one. Isaiah foretold that a virgin would give birth to God's Son. But who would have thought it truly possible—not Mary.

Grace is found in the results of Messiah's coming. We ought to be humbled to realize that God came in human form—not simply to be a sacrificial Lamb, but to experience life, to know us. We have a Savior that understands and knows our pressures, temptations, and trials. Yet, He is the provider of victory for us in the midst of it all.

Reread this passage with all of this in mind. God's favor and grace are upon us. Hallelujah!

SATURDAY—Eph. 2:3-14

On Christmas morning I am just like a little kid. I can't wait to see what is in my Christmas stocking or in the brightly wrapped packages under the tree. All of us think often about what we will get, and we all look forward to getting gifts at Christmas. This passage is one of the most beautiful in Scripture to describe God's gifting of life to us.

This passage uses the great word *lavished*. I love that word. It describes not only a gift of great value but also an intent that is motivated by love. Jesus Christ is God's gift to us. He was given not because we deserve it or have earned it, but because God desires to "bring all things in heaven and on earth together under one head, even Christ" (Eph. 1:10).

This week we have talked about how the prophets of old foretold of God's great gift to us. We have also been challenged to respond to His gift.

A Christian is one who has reached out and accepted God's free gift. If you have not accepted it, what a perfect time to accept God's free gift of salvation. This could be the best Christmas ever. If you have accepted Him, then thank God for His great love for you!

THE BETHLEHEM CANDLE

The Second Sunday of Advent
Key Word: HOPE

O come, O come, Hope of the Ages. Come through us to all who hunger for hope against great odds. May our hope be a beautiful Advent flame dancing in the darkness.

The second candle is violet. Each day light the prophecy candle and the Bethlehem candle. Be sure to repeat the names of each one.

The Bethlehem candle reminds us that Christ was born as a human baby in a specific place at a specific time in history. This is called Incarnation. One of the great mysteries of the Incarnation is that Jesus was both God and Man. Bethlehem reminds us of this.

O Little Town of Bethlehem*

O little town of Bethlehem,
    How still we see thee lie!
Above thy deep and dreamless sleep
    The silent stars go by.
Yet in thy dark streets shineth
    The everlasting Light;
The hopes and fears of all the years
    Are met in thee tonight.

For Christ is born of Mary;
    And gathered all above,
While mortals sleep, the angels keep
    Their watch of wond'ring love.
O morning stars, together
    Proclaim the holy birth;

---

*Words by Phillips Brooks (1835-93).

And praises sing to God, the King,
And peace to men on earth.

How silently, how silently
The wondrous Gift is giv'n!
So God imparts to human hearts
The blessing of His heav'n.
No ear may hear His coming;
But in this world of sin,
Where meek souls will receive Him still,
The dear Christ enters in.

O holy Child of Bethlehem,
Descend on us, we pray.
Cast out our sin, and enter in;
Be born in us today.
We hear the Christmas angels
The great glad tidings tell.
Oh, come to us, abide with us,
Our Lord, Emmanuel.

SUNDAY—Mic. 5:2; Matt. 2:1-6

Bethlehem had a long history. It was there that Jacob had buried Rachel. It was there that Ruth lived and married Boaz. But above all, Bethlehem was the home and the city of David. It was from the line of David that God was to send the great deliverer of His people. It was in Bethlehem that the Jews believed that the Messiah would be born.

What they didn't expect was that their Messiah did not come in a room of a beautiful palace. He was born across the tracks, on the poor side of town, in a stable—not a fit place for a king to be born, but a perfect place for the Son of God.

Bethlehem is a little town, an insignificant place. Jesus was born in that unimportant town, in a lowly place in that town. How fitting for the One who would understand us better than we understand ourselves.

When one thinks of Bethlehem, it is easy to be reminded that God sent His Son for all of lost humanity—not for just the wealthy or the beautiful, but for all.

MONDAY—John 6:25-59 (esp. v. 35)

Bethlehem means "the House of Bread." It stood in a fertile countryside. It was famous for its farming and production of wheat. How appropriate that Jesus, the Bread of Life, would be born there. The greatest tragedy of life is that our world has missed this fact. We scurry about looking for ways to feed, clothe, house, and entertain our bodies, when it is our souls that are starving to death.

Jesus came to be the Bread of Life. As this bread He seeks to sustain, satisfy, and nourish our lives. How does He do this? John 6:33 says, "For the bread of God is he who comes down from heaven and gives life to the world."

How long has it been since the Bread of Life has nourished your soul? During this holiday season this living bread is given to nourish and sustain us. Spend time with God, listen to Him, do what He says. That is how to be alive in Christ.

TUESDAY—Luke 2:1-7

The Emperor Augustus ordered that every 14 years an assessment be made of the population and resources of the empire. Quirinius, the governor of Syria, was the overseer of the land of Palestine. Everyone went to the place of his or her birth to be registered. Mary and Joseph set out for Bethlehem, since he was of the lineage of David. The trip took approximately three days and was over 75 miles in distance. Mary was in labor, so Joseph sought whatever shelter he could find. Since there was no room for them in the Bethlehem inn, Joseph found the next best thing. They joined the animals in their warm, dry dwelling. And so it was that the Prince of Peace was born amid the lowing of the cattle in the overcrowded town of Bethlehem.

I am confident that as Mary and Joseph gazed upon the face of their newborn child, they weren't upset because they were in a smelly stable. They must have felt as if they were the most fortunate of all the residents of Bethlehem, for they were gazing upon the King, the Son of God. It is amazing that when Jesus comes, He brings perspective even in a stable.

WEDNESDAY—Matt. 2:1-12

Nothing in the birth story is quite so fascinating as the journey and worship of the wise men. Who were these "wise guys"? Tradition has suggested that they were astrologers with religious interests, who lived in the Far East. They observed a strange star in the sky and decided that it signified a special happening, a royal birth. Tradition lends itself to the belief that there were three because of the number of gifts that were brought to the Christ child.

These wise men were not present at the stable but arrived from one to two years after the first sighting of the star. Matthew 2:11 suggests that Mary, Joseph, and Jesus lived in a house in Bethlehem.

The message of the story of the wise men is important. Christ is for men and women of all nations. Jesus was not just the King of the Jews but also the Redeemer of all lost humanity.

THURSDAY—Matt. 1:1-2

It may seem to us extraordinary that these men should set out from the East to find a king. But the climate of the day was such that there was a real feeling of expectation, a waiting for the coming of a world king. William Barclay says, "There had spread over all the Orient an old and established belief, that it was fated at that time for men coming from Judea to rule the world."* When Jesus came, the world of His

---

*William Barclay, *The Daily Study Bible: The Gospel of Matthew*, Vol. 1 (Edinburgh: St. Andrews Press, 1956), 18.

day was in an eagerness of expectation. Men were waiting for God. All eyes were focused on the Middle East, particularly Israel.

This is not unlike what we are experiencing today. All eyes are focused on the Middle East one more time. The reasons are different, yet similar. All of humanity is searching for a leader, a powerful ruler.

While we are celebrating the first coming of Jesus, it is a great time to look expectantly for the return of Jesus. Maranatha! Come quickly, Lord Jesus.

Pray for those in the Middle East during this time. Pray for their families. Pray for the rulers of the world. And wait with great expectation to see what God has in His plan.

FRIDAY—Matt. 2:13-23

The wise men go in search of this new King. They are uncertain where to go. They use excellent logic and head for the palace of King Herod. Obviously he must have fathered the next king. The results are unbelievable. Herod issues a decree to massacre all babies in Bethlehem two years and under.

This passage speaks of the protection of God. He warns the wise men not to return home the same way. He warns Joseph to hurry his family off to safety.

But this passage also is an illustration of what people will do to get rid of Jesus Christ. We see this evident everywhere. The commercialization of Christmas is appalling. People are working very hard to make sure that the true meaning of Christmas is nowhere to be found. It is time for Christians everywhere to stand up and be counted.

Discuss with your family how you can take a stand for Jesus that will make it clear to others whose you are.

SATURDAY—Rom. 12:9-21

The key word for this week has been *hope*. This passage in Paul's letter to the Romans is one of the greatest discussions on this subject. I particularly love the admonition found in verse 12, "Be joyful in hope." I have discovered this to be particularly important in the midst of my own dark valleys. Joy and hope don't seem to go together very well. But the truth is that they go together better than the proverbial "horse and carriage." Joy is founded in hope, and hope springs forth out of the joy in our hearts.

This holiday season I encourage you to experience the joy of the celebration of the birth of the Savior. Focus your hope on the things above. God has a wonderful plan for His children. I challenge you: feast on the Bread of Life, respond with joy from the depths of your soul, and look forward with great hope that the God who sent His Son for you is working faithfully in your life. And then take the hope challenge—spread hope wherever you go. This world needs it.

THE SHEPHERDS' CANDLE

Third Sunday of Advent
Key Word: JOY

Sing to the stars, O children of God, for Christmas is near. Make of each prayer and good deed a radiant gift of adoration to the stable-born Prince of Heaven and Earth.

The first candle is the prophecy candle. The second candle is the Bethlehem candle. The third Advent candle, the shepherds' candle, is pink to represent joy and celebration. Light all three candles; be sure to name each one. Remember, the candles remind us that Jesus is the Light of the World.

The shepherds were able to share in the joy of Jesus' birth. What a privilege. This week you will also get an opportunity to share in the results of the special birth.

While Shepherds Watched Their Flocks*

While shepherds watched their flocks by night,
All seated on the ground,
The angel of the Lord came down,
And glory shone around,
And glory shone around.

"Fear not," said he, for mighty dread
Had seized their troubled mind.
"Glad tidings of great joy I bring
To you and all mankind,
To you and all mankind."

---

*Words by Nahum Tate (1652—1715).

"To you, in David's town, this day,
Is born, of David's line,
The Savior, who is Christ the Lord;
And this shall be the sign,
And this shall be the sign:"

"The heav'nly Babe you there shall find
To human view displayed,
All meanly wrapped in swathing bands,
And in a manger laid,
And in a manger laid."

Thus spake the seraph, and forthwith
Appeared a shining throng
Of angels praising God on high,
Who thus addressed their song,
Who thus addressed their song:

"All glory be to God on high,
And to the earth be peace.
Goodwill henceforth from heav'n to men
Begin and never cease,
Begin and never cease!"

SUNDAY—Luke 2:8-20

It is simply wonderful that the initial announcement of the birth of the Messiah King, the Christ, would come to lowly shepherds. Shepherds were the lowest and most common of people because it was very difficult for them to keep the ceremonial laws and still care for their sheep. But it is to simple men of the fields that God's message first came.

As we read the Gospel accounts of the birth of Jesus, we are struck by the rough simplicity of His birth. We might have expected that the King of Kings would be born in a mansion or a palace. God saw fit to have His Son born in the common fashion, thus opening the door for all to come.

There is a story of a European monarch who would worry his court by disappearing and walking incognito among his people. When asked why he did this, his reply went something like this: "I can't rule unless I know how they live." I think that God must have thought much along these same lines. The letter to the Hebrews tells us Jesus knows who we are because He was, and still is, one of us. (See Heb. 2:11, 14-18.) I am glad that the Christmas story reminds us that this is true.

MONDAY—Luke 2:8-20

I have always been fascinated by the story "The Little Drummer Boy." I know that it is purely fictional, but I love the concept of offering music to the newborn King. In fact, during this time in Israel's history, when a child was born, local musicians often came to greet the new child with simple music. Jesus was born in secret in a stable in Bethlehem, so local musicians would not know to come and celebrate. However, it is exciting that God sent the greatest musicians of all, His angels, to herald the birth of His Son.

TUESDAY—Luke 2:8-20

The shepherds are a real inspiration to me. First, I am not surprised that they were frightened. Wouldn't you be if an angel appeared to you and started talking? The thing that amazes me is that they didn't faint. Second, they seem to know who sent the angel. These lowliest of their culture were expecting a Messiah. They were not surprised when God came through. Too often I miss little miracles in my life because I don't expect God to come through. Third, they responded right away. They didn't hesitate long, but headed for Bethlehem to check out this thing, which the angels had told them about. Fourth, this announcement may have seemed strange and almost improbable, but they betray no doubts, no questions, and no hesitation. They hasten to Bethlehem and there find everything exactly as had been told them. Their simple faith received a rich reward. Fifth, they didn't keep quiet but told everyone who would listen. I imagine that the chorus that the angels sang kept running through their minds and out of their mouths. Moved by a blessed faith to worship and glorify God, they became the first converts, first disciples, and first evangelists. Oh, for a simple faith.

WEDNESDAY—Luke 2:8-20

What happens when we see Jesus? The Scriptures say, "Mary treasured up all of these things and pondered them in her heart" (Luke 2:19). Her heart must have been ready to explode with the love she felt as a mother of a newborn, especially with the realization that she had indeed given life to the Son of God. How could she doubt when she heard the story of the shepherds? About Joseph, we have little information; but I am inclined to think that he was humbled by the awesome responsibility of being part of this most excellent plan. Later we see Joseph obediently following the warning of the angels to protect Jesus. When they saw Jesus, the shepherds responded with praises and glory to God.

My prayer is that more of us would really see Jesus. For when we do, we can't help but respond with praise and glory to our loving God. "For God so loved the world that he gave . . ." (John 3:16). Hallelujah!

THURSDAY—Ps. 100

I was a very young child when I first memorized this psalm. It still means a great deal to me. It is a call to praise God, to shout for joy. In the midst of the rapid pace of our lives, it is often hard to sense any joy at all. Look around you at the faces of the folks you see. Do their faces reflect any joy? We live in the wealthiest nation in the world. Yet we run here and there trying to find that magic "thing" that will finally bring us happiness. The sad thing is that it never does. The Bible tells us that real joy comes only from knowing Jesus. "It is he who made us, and we are his" (Ps. 100:3). When my daughter Sarah was two years old, an evangelist friend of mine asked her who she was. She very proudly grabbed the leg of my pants and said, "I am his daughter." There was real joy in her voice because she knew she belonged to somebody. Our joy comes from belonging to God. To whom do you belong?

FRIDAY—Luke 2:21-40

In this passage we see Jesus undergoing three Jewish ceremonies that every boy had to go through.

First is circumcision. This signified His identification with the people of God, the people of Abraham.

Second is the "Redemption of the Firstborn." Every firstborn male, both human and animal, was sacred to God. A sum of five shekels was given to the priests to redeem or buy back their firstborn son.

Third is purification. This was to purify the mother for uncleanness in childbirth. Mary and Joseph could only afford the sacrifice of the poor, which was "a pair of doves and two young pigeons" (Luke 2:24).

All three of these ceremonies show that a child is a gift from God.

God had promised Simeon, an old man, that he would see the Messiah before he died. When he saw Mary and Joseph and Jesus, he knew that this Child was more than an ordinary child. He knew that this was the Messiah. Simeon took Jesus and dedicated and blessed Him.

Jesus is more than a good man, a nice guy, and a prophet. He is the Messiah, the Savior of the world. Joy comes in seeing Him.

SATURDAY—Luke 2:39-40

Mary and Joseph have always been important figures throughout history. These simple verses portray to us the depth of character that these two people possess. Mary and Joseph were ready and willing to do everything that was necessary to help God fulfill His promise. Mary was willing to endure gossip, rejection, and the threat of death. Joseph was willing to suffer ridicule, embarrassment, and shame. They traveled to Bethlehem, endured birth in a stable, before they were married, and followed the prescribed procedures of their religion. Yet throughout it all you don't hear a "Why me, God?" or "This isn't fair" or "Can You make this a little easier?" No, in fact, we see only faithful obedience. When I look at these two selfless folks, I am challenged. Lord, help us to be more faithful.

THE ANGELS' CANDLE

Fourth Sunday of Advent
Key Word: LOVE

God, You who so loved the world that You sent Your Son to live in human flesh, help us be Your living gifts of love to family, friends, and strangers. Amen.

The first candle is the prophecy candle. The second candle is the Bethlehem candle. Third is the shepherds' candle. The last is the angels' candle. Light all four candles, repeating their names. The angels' candle, which is violet, tells us that the angels were messengers proclaiming Christ's birth to Mary and the shepherds.

Hark! The Herald Angels Sing*

Hark! The herald angels sing:
"Glory to the newborn King!
Peace on earth, and mercy mild;
God and sinners reconciled."
Joyful, all ye nations, rise;
Join the triumph of the skies;
With th'angelic hosts proclaim,
"Christ is born in Bethlehem."
Hark! The herald angels sing,
"Glory to the newborn King."

Christ, by highest heav'n adored;
Christ, the everlasting Lord!
Long desired, behold Him come,
Finding here His humble home.
Veiled in flesh the Godhead see;

---

*Words by Charles Wesley (1707-88).

Hail th'incarnate Deity!
Pleased as man with men to dwell,
Jesus, our Immanuel!
Hark! The herald angels sing,
"Glory to the newborn King."

Hail, the heav'n-born Prince of Peace!
Hail, the Sun of Righteousness!
Light and life to all He brings,
Ris'n with healing in His wings.
Mild He lays His glory by,
Born that man no more may die.
Born to raise the sons of earth,
Born to give them second birth.
Hark! The herald angels sing,
"Glory to the newborn King."

(Special Note: If Christmas Eve and Christmas come during this week, turn ahead to those pages.)

SUNDAY—Luke 1:26-38

The chief angel startled Mary with the greeting, "Greetings, you who are highly favored! The Lord is with you" (Luke 1:28). After she gained her composure, Gabriel delivered his famous message: "You have found favor with God. You will be with child and give birth to a son, and you are to give him the name Jesus. He will be great and will be called the Son of the Most High" (vv. 30-32). The messenger indicated that the birth would be one of great importance, in fact the most important birth ever. Mary would bring forth the long-awaited One, the Messiah.

Mary, like any devout Jewish woman, would love to be the mother of the Deliverer of the Jewish people. But this would be scandalous, for she was unmarried. And what would Joseph think?

After evaluating the situation, she realized that the risk was in God's hands, and her response was, "I am the Lord's servant . . . May it be to me as you have said" (v. 38).

It would be something to have a visit from one of God's heavenly messengers. But, it would be quite another matter when that messenger gives you news that could cost you your life and at the very least drastically change your plans. But Mary's example reverberates across the centuries. Her yes is an encouragement to us to say yes to God when He invades our ordered world and turns it upside down. We learn from Mary that God's plan is always best.

MONDAY—Isa. 40:10-11; 53:2-7

What a powerful passage! Christmas is a day of *hope*. Earl Lee once said, "Christmas is not only a day in December; it is every time our tears are wiped away; every time new hope arises like a star in our dark night of the spirit; every time a sinner is saved by grace; every time a heart is filled with the Holy Spirit; every time a Blood-washed pilgrim enters into life eternal!"* This is the great hope of the gospel; this is what the name *Jesus* means to a lost and dying world.

The real Christmas message is that God would save lost humanity, and to Him this saving was worth any cost it would require. Hallelujah!

TUESDAY—Matt. 1:18-25

The message of the angel to both Joseph and Mary is "do not be afraid" (Matt. 1:20; Luke 1:30). I imagine that would be a very important thing to be told when confronted with the presence of an angel. These heavenly messengers had the privilege to carry the greatest message ever told.

At Christmas there is no more fitting message than "do not be

---

*Earl Lee, notes in my Bible from a message I heard on tape from Pasadena First Church of the Nazarene.

afraid." With the world so filled with fear and foreboding, it is exciting to know that the message the angel brought is as important to us today as it was to Joseph. How do we confront the fears of our day? It is only possible as we listen carefully to the message of the angel. He said, "Do not be afraid." Why shouldn't we fear? The answer is, because Jesus has come. What is so special about Jesus? He is "the Lamb that was slain from the creation of the world" (Rev. 13:8). He is the One who desires to carry our burdens, concerns, and fears. Whatever your fears, Jesus, the Babe of Bethlehem, is ready to carry them.

WEDNESDAY—Heb. 1

Christmas is the celebration of the most wonderful gift in all of human history—God sent His Son to earth to redeem our world. The story is incredible, yet simple and beautiful. No wonder people's lives seem to change at this remarkable time of the year.

Our families have discovered that celebrating the birth of Jesus in a memorable way doesn't just happen. Unless preparations are made beforehand, we are overcome by Christmas chaos rather than the joy and peace we want to fill our homes. The angels spoke of joy and peace. With a little planning it is possible in the midst of this fast-paced season to allow the joy and peace of the season to reign.

I recommend creating some Christmas traditions that focus on togetherness and slowing down—reading the Christmas story together, talking about a favorite Christmas, singing carols, and so on. You will find Christmas to be very special. Focus on love—God's love for us and our love for others.

THURSDAY—Luke 1:11-25

Talk about a surprise, this was a surprise for Zechariah. If Advent means anything, it means that we should get ready for, and wait patiently for, surprises. Nothing is more surprising than the birth of the Son of God to a pious Jewish girl and her carpenter spouse.

Many of us love surprises at Christmas. I never want to know what I am getting. But in life we don't care much for surprises. We're great for planning, for trying to work life all out in advance. We will marry on this date, have this many children, make this much money per year, live in this kind of house, take a vacation each summer for this many days, retire at this age—and no surprises, please. Just in case there are some surprises, we have insurance policies to run interference for us.

Fat chance. Remember: surprises are holy. The way we tend to live, a surprise is about the only place God can find some elbow room, some space to shake up our lives so we'll realize how deep is His love for us. The God of Advent is waiting. "Father, help me respect the surprises in my life and be sensitive to Your presence in them."

FRIDAY—Luke 1:39 ff.

Elizabeth, the cousin of Mary, was unable to conceive a child. She and her husband, Zechariah, had prayed earnestly for this special gift from God. A miracle happened. Elizabeth became pregnant. At the time that Mary visited her, Elizabeth was already in the sixth month of her pregnancy that would soon end with the birth of John the Baptist. She welcomed the visit of Mary—Mary who was pregnant with Jesus.

The movement of John in his mother's womb has been interpreted in tradition as his baptism. This may be simply a legend, but something happened. There was a miraculous recognition within the womb of Elizabeth. Mary and Elizabeth recognized one another as examples of individuals living in God's special grace. The joy of Mary, the woman blessed beyond all others, overflowed to Elizabeth, the sterile woman at last fulfilled by this pregnancy. I like to think that even today, holy people who are filled with God's presence still cause their brothers and sisters who are filled with that same presence to be moved with sudden joy as they recognize the existence of the living Christ in one another.

SATURDAY—Luke 1:42*b*

Christmas is first and foremost a story about a newborn Baby. It is amazing how children especially perceive the story of Christmas. Leo Buscaglia, in *Seven Stories of Christmas Love*, tells of being responsible for a school Christmas program. Mary and Joseph came onstage to strains of "Silent Night," seated themselves on flour sacks, leaned against each other, and fell asleep. Other children were dressed as sheep and cows making animal sounds. An angel, with wings drooping, entered carrying Baby Jesus and placed Him on the straw, then quoted the Luke 2 ending: "wrapped in swaddling clothes and laid him in a manger." The boy playing Joseph awakened. Leo doesn't know what possessed the boy, but he said, "Mary! Wake up and see what you had during the night!"*

We all think as parents that our own newborn babies are special, and they are. Actually, in truth, most newborn babies are pretty much alike—red and wrinkled. But Mary's baby really was special. Elizabeth said, "Blessed is the child" (Luke 1:42*b*). What made Jesus a blessed baby? Reflect on this thought as you discuss Christmas.

---

*Leo Buscaglia, *Seven Stories of Christmas Love* (Thorofare, N.J.: SLACK Inc., 1992), 101.

THE CHRIST CANDLE

Advent

On Christmas Eve, light the four Advent candles, repeating their names: prophecy, Bethlehem, shepherds', and angels'. Then light the center Christ candle.

The Christ candle symbolizes Christ's presence in our world. Now all the candles are burning. Christ is born! What a cause for rejoicing!

Silent Night!*

Silent night! Holy night!
All is calm, all is bright
Round yon virgin mother and Child.
Holy Infant, so tender and mild,
Sleep in heavenly peace,
Sleep in heavenly peace.

Silent night! Holy night!
Shepherds quake at the sight.
Glories stream from heaven afar;
Heav'nly hosts sing Alleluia!
Christ, the Savior, is born!
Christ, the Savior, is born!

Silent night! Holy night!
Son of God, love's pure light
Radiant beams from Thy holy face,
With the dawn of redeeming grace,

---

*Words by Joseph Mohr (1792—1848), German; stanzas 1 and 3 translated by John F. Young (1820-85); translator of stanzas 2 and 4 unknown.

Jesus, Lord, at Thy birth;
Jesus, Lord, at Thy birth.

Silent night! Holy night!
Wondrous star, lend thy light;
With the angels let us sing,
Alleluia to our King;
Christ, the Savior, is born!
Christ, the Savior, is born!

CHRISTMAS EVE—Matt. 1:18-25

"You are to give him the name Jesus" (Matt. 1:21). In the history of the Jews this was a grand name. It was the same as Joshua, the successor to Moses. The priest who aided Zerubbabel in the restoration of the Temple following the Exile also bore that name.

The name Jesus meant "Yahweh (God) is Salvation." The name gained real significance from the mouth of Gabriel: "Because he will save his people from their sins."

William Barclay says, "Jesus enables us to see what God is and what man ought to be; Jesus opens the eyes of our minds so that we can see the truth of God for us; Jesus is the creating power come among men; Jesus is the recreating power which can release the souls of man from the death of sin."*

For those of us who have learned to rely upon Jesus, there is beauty and mystery in His name. It is a name that is warm and inviting. He is a friend who is closer than a brother. The greatest truth of scripture is that God is like Jesus. I hope you know Him.

CHRISTMAS DAY—Matt. 1:22-23

I love the name Immanuel. Immanuel means "God with us." It carries with it three ideas that are extremely helpful.

*William Barclay, *The Daily Study Bible: The Gospel of Matthew*, Vol. 1 (Edinburgh: St. Andrews Press, 1956), 13-14.

First, Christ came to dwell among His people. I am so grateful that God sent His Son to experience what it is like to be human. Read Phil. 2:1-11 for a better understanding of what Jesus did. He became the God-Man forever to redeem us.

Second, Christ came to interact with His people. As we read the Gospels, we are struck with the way Jesus interacted with people. His was a ministering love. That same love He showed then, He still shows today.

Third, Christ continues to be with His people. He intercedes for us—He never leaves nor forsakes. Immanuel—God with us. Thank You, Lord.

Have a Merry CHRISTmas!

(God bless you this holiday season. May it be the best ever because you have put the Christ of Christmas as the Head of your home. GW)

APPENDIX 3

Hanging of the Greens

(This is simply one example of this special service. The order of the service is given first, and an explanation of each section then follows.)

A Service for the Hanging of the Greens

WELCOME

CALL TO WORSHIP

Leader: "Arise, shine; for your light has come, and the glory of the LORD has risen upon you. . . . Lift up your eyes round about and see." [Isa. 60:1, 4, NASB]

All: "'Sing and rejoice . . . For behold, I am coming and I will dwell in your midst,' says the LORD." [Zech. 2:10, NKJV]

Leader: "As with gladness men of old / Did the guiding star behold; / As with joy they hailed its light, / Leading onward, beaming bright; / So, most gracious Lord, may we / Evermore be led to Thee."

THE MEANING OF THE SERVICE

THE ADVENT WREATH

Scripture: Jer. 23:5-6

Hymn: "O, Come, O Come, Emmanuel"

RINGING OF THE CHRISTMAS BELLS

Scripture: Ps. 150

Hymn: "Come On, Ring Those Bells"

THE HANGING OF THE SANCTUARY GREENS

Scripture: Isa. 9:6-7; Luke 2:29-32

Hymn: "The First Noel"

CAROLING

Hymn: "Joy to the World"

THE MISTLETOE

OFFERING

THE CHRISTMAS TREE

Hymn: "O Little Town of Bethlehem"

<table>
<tr><td>

THE NATIVITY
Hymn: "Silent Night"

THE ANGELS
Hymn: "Angels from the Realms
of Glory"

THE GIFTS
Hymn: "We Three Kings"

</td><td>

THE CANDLES
Solo: "O Holy Night"

BENEDICTION
Hymn: "O Come, All Ye Faithful"

</td></tr>
</table>

Hanging of the Greens (the Service Explained)

(The large decorations should already be in place prior to the service—this speeds up the service and keeps it flowing nicely. I usually had the tree in place and large wreaths, and so forth. Small items that can be placed during the service should be held until time to place them.)

Welcome

Welcome to the hanging of the greens. This is a very special festival of popular Christmas customs. The observance of the hanging of the greens is an old English custom of decorating the house with evergreens and other festive trappings for the Christmas season. The service is packed with meaning as together we learn the significance of the various traditions that make up our seasons of Advent and Christmas. (*Turn the lights down.*)

Call to Worship

Leader: "Arise, shine; for your light has come, and the glory of the LORD has risen upon you. . . . Lift up your eyes round about and see." [Isa. 60:1, 4, NASB]

All: "'Sing and rejoice . . . For behold, I am coming and I will dwell in your midst,' says the LORD." [Zech. 2:10, NKJV]

Leader: "As with gladness men of old / Did the guiding star behold; / As with joy they hailed its light, / Leading onward, beaming bright; / So, most gracious Lord, may we / Evermore be led to Thee."*

---

*William Dix, "As with Gladness Men of Old" (1860).

Invocation

Introduction

The truth is, there never was any Christmas before Christ came! Year after year the evergreen trees grew in the woods, but nobody came to get them. Boys and girls grew up into men and women with never a single Christmas carol, Christmas gift, or Christmas tree.

God saw the sorrow and sin that were upon the earth, so He decided to make himself known in a new way. God decided to come to earth—not in royal robes of splendor—but as a humble little baby to be born in a barn, to grow up in a little out-of-the-way village with other boys and girls and to live among people to teach them about God's will for their lives.

The Advent Wreath
Scripture: Jer. 23:5-6

Advent means "the coming" and is the name given to the four-week period just before Christmas. One of the loveliest customs to mark this season is the lighting of the candles on the Advent wreath.

The wreath consists of a circle of evergreens that lie flat on a surface, with three purple candles and one rose candle around the circle, and one white candle in the center.

The circle represents the eternal nature of God. The evergreens represent everlasting life. Purple is the royal color and the symbol of humility and penitence; rose is the color of joy and happiness, the symbol of hope; white refers to the Lord's purity and perfection. These candles represent the four Sundays preceding Christmas, one candle being lit each Sunday, with the white candle being lit on Christmas Eve.

The first candle is the candle of *prophecy*. It calls attention to the prophecies of the coming Savior. It calls us to prepare for Christmas by prayerfully humbling ourselves before God. The second candle represents *Bethlehem*, the lowly place of the birth of our Savior. The third candle is the *shepherds'* candle. It is pink, representing joy and celebration. The shepherds remind us that we share in the joy of Jesus' birth. The fourth candle is the *angels'* candle. This reminds us of the messengers who came to proclaim Christ's birth. The fifth candle is the *Christ* candle, and it symbolizes Christ's presence in our world. Christ is born! Hallelujah!

Hymn: "O Come, O Come, Emmanuel"

The Ringing of the Christmas Bells
Scripture: Ps. 150

Hundreds of years before the first Christmas, bells announced happy and sad events. The high priests of the ancient Hebrews wore robes decorated with tiny golden bells, and they rang handbells at their ceremonies.

During the sixth century, bells appeared in Christian churches. On Christmas Eve they announced the birth of Jesus. By the Middle Ages, bells became an established part of the Christmas season.

Charles Wesley is said to have composed the carol "Hark! The Herald Angels Sing" after listening to Christmas chimes. Bells were never so welcome as at Christmas, when they pealed forth the message of peace and joy.

(Tell people that at the conclusion of singing we will ring our bells in unison—be sure and tell them ahead of time to bring bells to this service.)

Hymn: "Come On, Ring Those Bells"

The Hanging of the Sanctuary Greens
Scripture: Isa. 9:6-7; Luke 2:29-32

HOLLY—"CHRIST'S THORN"

Sacred long before Christ's birth, holly was believed to have protective qualities against evil forces. In the church age in Scandinavia, it came to be known as Christ's thorn, probably in reference to the crown of thorns Jesus wore at His crucifixion. Old Christmas customs say that holly was to be brought into the church on Christmas Eve. It was to adorn the church until Twelfth Night, or Epiphany, when the arrival of the wise men is traditionally celebrated. With its classic green and red Christmas colors, holly's symbolism is one of eternal life and domestic peace.

WREATHS AND GREENS

Wreaths, with their circular shape, and evergreen boughs have long symbolized eternity. They have been used throughout the world in churches for decoration. Their usage probably originated in pre-Christian Rome where they were used in celebrations of victory, such as sporting events.

Even after Christ's birth the Roman Empire continued to worship their pagan gods. Cruel punishment would befall those brave early Christians who chose to openly worship Christ. In December, when other Romans celebrated their religion, Christians chose to celebrate the birth of Jesus of Nazareth. To avoid notice, these followers of Christ would deck their homes like the pagan Romans, with evergreens and wreaths.

As Christianity spread, these first customs prevailed, signifying everlasting life, joy, and the victory that is ours in Christ. Today wreaths represent God's eternal nature and His endless love. It seems that wherever you live, this is the season to deck the halls.

Hymn: "The First Noel"

The Custom of Caroling

Francis of Assisi taught his people to "tell of your Christmas joy in songs." He is called the father of the Christmas carol. Francis founded a religious order called the Franciscans. His brothers wrote many lovely Christmas carols and carried the custom of carol singing across Europe.

Most of these early carols were sung outdoors by strolling carolers. Lighted windows signaled the singers to stop. Caroling was thought to bring good fortune to homes.

The first printed book of carols appeared in 1521. Since then many old carols have been collected and printed.

Hymn: "Joy to the World"

The Custom of the Mistletoe

Used to signify goodwill, mistletoe is hung over doorways. Furthermore, early Christians in England would give each other a sacred kiss of peace and goodwill under the mistletoe when they received Communion. In time lovers began sealing their vows beneath the shiny leaves of the plant.

Early Christians called this greenery "all heal" and saw it as symbolic of the healing power of the Lord. It was considered so sacred that when two enemies chanced to meet beneath it in the wood where it grew wild, a truce would be declared. Their weapons would be put down, and they would kiss as a show of reconciliation.

Therefore, the mistletoe is a symbol to us of reconciliation and commitment.

The Christmas Tree
Scripture: Luke 2:8-22

Deeply rooted in old legends, the Christmas tree is one of the most loved and widespread of the Christmas customs. One legend goes back to the time of Christ's birth.

Herod had sent out the decree that the Holy Child was to be found and killed. It is said that Mary, Joseph, and Jesus escaped detection as they hid behind an old evergreen.

Others maintain that the German church reformer, Martin Luther, began the custom. Apparently, Luther was so inspired by the tall beauty of evergreens against a starry sky that he brought one home to his family. He placed lighted candles in its branches to symbolize the star perched in the heavens over Bethlehem.

The first authenticated record of a Christmas tree is in a German book dated 1604. By the 19th century, the custom had spread throughout Germany to Austria, Finland, Scandinavia, and France. At that time immigrants were flooding into America bringing with them a wealth of culture and holiday customs.

A symbolic value of the Christmas tree is as rich as its heritage. The French believe it represents the tree in the Garden of Eden and so decorated it with apples. To others, the tree symbolized the Cross with the top pointing to the heaven. Some authorities say the Christmas tree corresponds to the Jewish festival of Hanukkah, or the Festival of Lights, in which a nine-branched menorah, or candelabra, is used. These scholars see the Christmas tree to be the fulfillment of this custom with the tree representing the Cross and eternal life; and the lights, Christ, the Light of the World.

Today most Christmas trees in America are loaded with ornaments, lights, dazzling balls, angels, tinsel, and beloved family heirlooms—the symbols of the joy of many lands. The Christmas tree helps us remember and celebrate the coming of the long-awaited Messiah, our promised Savior and blessed hope.

(*This is an excellent time for people to place the personal ornaments they have brought with them upon the tree. Make sure that large things like strings of lights, garlands, and so forth, have already been placed upon the tree.*)

Hymn: "O Little Town of Bethlehem"

The Nativity

In Italy Christmas centers around the Nativity scene or *presepio*. This moving custom originated in 1223 with Francis of Assisi. He was so affected by a visit to Bethlehem, the birthplace of our Lord, that he decided to reenact the event with villagers to play the various roles and with live animals in the barn. The Christ child rather than being represented by a real child was symbolized by a wax candle that signified the Holy Child as the Light of the World.

The Nativity is a physical reminder of humble beginnings; a barn and a manger where the King of Kings and Lord of Lords made His first appearance to the world for which He would one day lay down His life.

Hymn: "Silent Night"

The Angels

It should not surprise us that we decorate our homes and Christmas trees with angels. Throughout the ages God has sent angels to play a part in each believer's life.

The responsibilities of angels include proclamation and declaration. They played a major role in the Christmas story even before the birth of Christ. Zechariah was the first to experience an angelic encounter having to do with the Lord's birth. Zechariah and his wife, Elizabeth, were childless when the angel Gabriel appeared to him. Gabriel said they would have a son, John the Baptist, who would prepare the way for the coming Messiah.

Mary was engaged to Joseph when the angel Gabriel told her she had favor with God, would conceive by the Holy Spirit, and bear a child who would be the Son of God. Joseph was preparing for a quiet divorce, as was the Jewish custom in such matters, when he had an angelic visitation. An angel appeared to him in a dream telling him not to be afraid to marry the girl. The Child she carried was the promised Emmanuel—"God with us."

Later in Bethlehem an angel appeared to the shepherds in the field, saying, "Fear not: for, behold, I bring you good tidings of great joy, which shall be to all people. For unto you is born this day in the city of David a Saviour, which is Christ the Lord" (Luke 2:10-11, KJV).

Hymn: "Angels from the Realms of Glory"

The Gifts
Scripture: Matt. 1:1-12

In the Middle Ages, children's gifts often came in bundles of three. There was something rewarding, something useful, and something for discipline.

For most Christians, a Christmas gift is a symbol of the gifts taken to Bethlehem by the wise men. They represented the Christ child with three gifts, each foretelling something Christ would become: gold—a king; frankincense—a high priest; and myrrh—a martyr.

Hymn: "We Three Kings"

The Candles

For all ancient people, light meant new life. People of the Middle Ages put lighted candles in their windows on Christmas Eve to guide the Christ child on His way. No stranger was turned away, for, who knew, he might be the Christ child in disguise.

Every Christmas, glowing candles appear in windows, on fireplace mantels, and at dinner tables. Lighted candles are symbols, not only of Christmas but of Easter and birthdays too. Some form of light has marked all human occasions of joy.

The use of candles was originally an Italian custom, symbolic of Christ. "I am the light of the world. Whoever follows me will never walk in darkness, but will have the light of life" (John 8:12).

At first tallow candles were used. Now wax candles are preferred as a symbol of Mary's purity, for wax is the product of virgin bees. It is said that the wax represents Christ's body; the wick, His soul; and the flame, His divine nature. Christ is the Light of the World!

(*Everyone has a candle. The first candles are lit by the pastor. Each one in turn lights another's candle until the entire sanctuary is lit with candles.*)

Solo: "O Holy Night"

Closing Prayer/Benediction

Hymn: "O Come, All Ye Faithful"

APPENDIX 4

Christmas Eve Services

Christmas Eve Vespers

CALL TO WORSHIP

Hymn: "I Heard the Bells on Christmas Day"

INVOCATION

WELCOME

Pastor or worship leader

Hymn: "O Come, All Ye Faithful"

PROPHECY—Prepare

Isaiah 7:14 *(printed and unison)*

Hymn: "O Come, O Come, Emmanuel"

Isaiah 9:6 *(unison)*

Hymn: "Hallelujah! What a Savior!"

BETHLEHEM—Hope

Mic. 5:2 *(unison)*

Special Music: "Bethlehem Morn"

Hymn: "O Little Town of Bethlehem"

SHEPHERDS—Joy

Luke 2:8-20

Children's Story: "The Crippled Lamb"

Hymn: "While Shepherds Watched Their Flocks"

ANGELS—Love

Luke 1:26-38

Hymn: "Hark! The Herald Angels Sing"

THE CHRIST CANDLE—

Advent/Coming

Matt. 1:18-25

Hymn: "Child in a Manger"

Special: "Mary, Did You Know?"

Hymn: "Silent Night"

CHRISTMAS—

The King Has Come

Special: "He Is Messiah"

Hymn: "Joy to the World"

BENEDICTION

Christmas Eve Family Worship

(a suggested service)

(The family gathers around the fireplace or near the Christmas tree or other suitable Christmas center.)

Sing together: "Silent Night"

Father: This is the most wonderful night of the year. It is the time we celebrate the birthday of Jesus.

Mother: Let us hear again the beautiful story of the birth of our Savior.

Father: Hundreds of years before Jesus was born, God promised through the prophet Isaiah that a Savior would be born: "Unto us a child is born, unto us a son is given: and the government shall be upon his shoulder: and his name shall be called Wonderful, Counselor, The mighty God, The everlasting Father, The Prince of Peace" (Isa. 9:6, KJV).

Children: Let's read Luke's story about Mary and the shepherds and the angels.

All read: *(Everyone can read a few verses until it is finished.)* Luke 2:1-20

Sing: "O Little Town of Bethlehem"

Children: We must have the "wise men" story to make it like Christmas.

Father: You know the wise men didn't arrive to worship the infant King until two years later, but their story is still part of the Christ event. This is a story of great men who traveled a great distance to worship the king.

Mother *(Reads Matt. 2:1-15)*

Children: We know a verse that tells about God's great love in sending Jesus. "For God so loved the world, that he gave his only begotten Son, that whosoever believeth in him should not perish, but have everlasting life" (John 3:16, KJV).

Sing: "Joy to the World"

Father or Mother *(Leads in prayer of thanksgiving for Jesus. All pray the Lord's Prayer together.)*

APPENDIX 5

Ash Wednesday Service

ORGAN VOLUNTARY
"Unto Thee I Cry, Lord Jesus"—J. S. Bach

GREETING
The grace of the Lord Jesus Christ be with you
And also with you.
Bless the Lord who forgives all our sins.
God's mercy endures forever.

OPENING PRAYER (Unison)
"O God, maker of everything and judge of all that You have made, from the dust of the earth You have formed us and from the dust of the earth You would raise us up. By the redemptive power of the Cross, create in us clean hearts and put within us a new spirit, that we may repent of our sins and lead lives worthy of Your calling; through Jesus Christ, our Lord. Amen."

HYMN

PASSING OF THE PEACE
(Greet one another with words and signs of reconciliation and love)

Scripture: Joel 2:1-1, 12-17

Psalm: Ps. 51:1-17

Gospel: Matt. 6:1-6, 16-21

MESSAGE

INVITATION TO OBSERVANCE OF LENTEN DISCIPLINE
A brief silence is kept

PRAYER OF CONFESSION
"Gracious, forgiving God, we confess, through the faith that is in our hearts, our trust in You. We also confess that we have not always loved You as we should, often failing to be loyal, choosing our own way in-

stead of Yours. In our rebellion we have ignored those in need, and have not loved our neighbors. Hear our prayer, and forgive us, that we may know the freedom of joyful obedience; we pray through Jesus Christ our Lord. Amen."

A TIME OF SILENT PRAYER

ASSURANCE OF FORGIVENESS

Hymn: "Amazing Grace"

THANKSGIVING OVER ASHES

IMPOSITION OF ASHES

Those who wish are invited to come forward at this time and receive the mark of ashes as a sign of forgiveness and new life. The old has died. The new has come. *(As participants come forward, the ministers put ashes in the shape of a cross on their head—be sure to mix ashes with oil so they stick.)*

PRAYER OF THANKSGIVING

THE LORD'S PRAYER

Hymn: "When I Survey the Wondrous Cross"

DISMISSAL WITH BLESSING

All may depart in silence.

APPENDIX 6

∞

PASSION WEEK

Maundy Thursday
Living Last Supper

A dramatic presentation of the Last Supper can be a meaningful experience for actors and audience alike. There are many scripts that can be purchased. I recommend that you enter the key words Living Last Supper into a search engine on the World Wide Web and you will find numerous choices.

The following is a suggestion to help you create and write your own script if you choose not to purchase one.

The Living Last Supper

(The following to be read as each disciple enters.)

ANDREW

Commitment came quickly for Andrew, who was the first to follow Jesus. He was nearby when John the Baptist baptized Jesus in the River Jordan. He did not demand a prominent position but rather was satisfied to be a close friend of Jesus. No one needed to praise Andrew for his devotion. His spiritual strength, human gentleness, and warm love were ever present. When there was a need, Andrew was there. He was always available to give helpful advice.

John the Baptist introduced Jesus to the nation; Andrew is noted for introducing Jesus to individuals. He brought his brother, Peter, to meet this fascinating young Teacher. Once he brought a young lad with a lunch to feed a multitude. He introduced Greeks to Jesus. In fact, Patros, in Greece, was the place where Andrew preached for the last time. Aigeatis, the governor of Patros, became enraged at Andrew for his preaching and ordered him to stand trial before the tribunal in an attempt to do away with the Christian faith.

Andrew remained tied to a cross with thick ropes for three days. Though the cost seems astounding, it did not seem too much for Andrew, whose love for Christ was heard in his last words. "Would Father, that I had time to teach truth to my murderers, accept me, O Christ Jesus, whom I saw, whom I love, and in whom I am. Accept my spirit in peace in your eternal realm."*

PETER

Peter found fishing for men as exciting for him as fishing for fish had been. His commitment was strong. Peter is the impulsive one, and this often led him down paths of personal sorrow and destruction. Although Paul would later outshine Peter as the spokesman for the new faith, Peter always remained in the affection of the early Christians as the first among the great Christians.

Peter's brash, fiery personality was the expression of a rare combination of courage and cowardice; of great strength and regrettable instability. Christ was a frequent guest in Peter's Capernaum home and was able to change this man, whose nature was as unstable as water, into a man with the consistency of a rock.

Peter, whose testimony of faith was the rock upon which Christ intended to build His Church, had an exquisite sense of sin. He sinned grievously as did Judas: Judas sold Jesus, and Peter cursed Him. There is no essential difference, except, Peter repented and Judas did not.

After nine months chained to a post in an underground cell, Peter was crucified head down. During his nine-month ordeal, Peter's magnificent spirit remained undaunted. It was flamed with the fervor

---

*"Andrew," BiblePath.Com, http://www.biblepath.com/andrew.html.

of his noble soul, proclaiming the glory of God, through His Son, Jesus Christ.

History tells us that in spite of all the suffering Peter was subjected to, he converted his jailers, Processus and Martinianus, and 47 others. Earlier in his pilgrimage Peter saw his wife martyred. He rejoiced because of her summons home to be with the Lord. He called to her encouragingly saying, "Remember the Lord."

JAMES, THE SON OF ZEBEDEE

James was the elder brother of John. He was a member of the inner circle of Jesus with Peter and John. He was the first to suffer martyrdom for his belief in Christ, thus fulfilling the prophecy of our Lord that he, too, should drink of the cup of the Master. The tone and style of James's death was due merely to suspicion of illegal activities.

James brought with him a contentment that enabled him to sense the slightest heartbreak or joy in Jesus. This knowledge, closeness, and sensitivity made James very dear to Jesus.

JOHN

As John walked closely by the side of the Master, he became transformed. His commitments brought about a change—a change from a son of thunder to an apostle of love. Hotheaded, warmhearted, eager, devoted, courageous to the end—John was known as the beloved disciple.

It was John who remained at the Cross; the only disciple.

It was John to whom Jesus entrusted His mother.

It was John who lived so close to the heartbeat of Jesus that he instantly recognized Him after His resurrection, a great act of faith.

It was John who preached the gospel and established churches long after Jesus left them and other disciples were killed.

John died a natural death, but his cross was found in his deep love and devotion, which made it possible for this beloved disciple to accomplish the unusual for his Master. In his last days John may have expressed his spirit by saying:

"Little children, love one another! . . . And if this alone be done, it is enough!"*

PHILIP

Philip was an educated young man, not willing to accept life only on the basis of feeling and emotion. Philip's commitment came after serious scrutiny when he found the message of the Master able to stand the test of investigation. From that commitment on, Philip remained practical with his feet on the ground but willing to take the risk of trusting the Master.

The Greek influence, which Philip had, was useful to the Master, who commanded that His gospel be taken to the Greek as well as the Jew. Philip recognized the power of the Lord and used it effectively to heal the sick, to cast out demons, and to show the way to the hungry of heart. Philip's service to the Master came in time and talent, as a powerful and vital man in bringing others to meet Christ.

He was stoned to death at the age of 87.

BARTHOLOMEW

Bartholomew, also called Nathanael, broke all the rules of tradition in exchange for the personal involvement he felt necessary to reach people. He was a man of vision; sometimes very different and unusual. By his conversion, the Master made use of this quality. Jesus recognized and used the creativeness in Bartholomew, and thus many spiritual ideas were made known. He went as far as India and Turkey with his purpose.

His steps were slow on the way to meet the Master. Perhaps he had

---

*"John (Son of Zebedee)," BiblePath.Com, http://www.biblepath.com/john1.html.

a premonition of his own unusual death he soon would experience. For a life given to Jesus, Bartholomew was flayed alive and crucified.

MATTHEW

Matthew, also called Levi, had been a tax collector prior to following Jesus. Perhaps he was the least likely person to make a commitment for service, for he had to give up much to become a disciple. He was educated and not well liked by the people. But Jesus in His great wisdom looked into the heart of the man and said, "Follow me." And the man we know as Matthew arose, forsook all that he had, and followed Jesus.

In his preaching, Matthew, like the other apostles, incurred the wrath of the Jewish establishment and was forced to turn to the Gentiles who gave him a more ready hearing. Matthew's love and service came to an end when he was burned to death. His testimony will live through the ages, "Not as I will, but as thou wilt" (Matt. 26:39, KJV).

THOMAS

Thomas, the pessimist, the doubter, or in fact was he the realist? Thomas possessed a nature that contained within it certain conflicting elements, which were difficult to reconcile. He possessed little natural buoyancy of spirit and was inclined often to look at life with icy coolness or despondency. Yet, Thomas was a man of indomitable courage and unselfishness. He combined a perpetual faith in the teaching of Jesus with a sincere love for Jesus, the Teacher.

Despite the difficulty Thomas had believing in the Resurrection, Jesus was able to use Thomas's spirit to speak to all humankind, when Jesus said, "Because thou hast seen me, thou hast believed: blessed are they that have not seen, and yet have believed" (John 20:29, KJV).

In the early days Thomas maintained a personality intent on gloom and doubt, yet he was a believer just the same. He did not have a wicked heart of unbelief; he was a man who struggled against his doubts and was ready to abandon them when he could. He became fearless in Christ and became a great builder of churches. Legend says he went to India, where to this day they consider him the great church planter of the cause of Christ. He also was a missionary to North Africa. While kneeling in prayer, he was mortally wounded by a shower of arrows and finally killed with a lance.

JAMES THE LESS

Originally part of the revolutionary zealots, James was a sensitive and emotional young man. He had been overcome with grief at the events leading up to the Last Supper. Jesus knew that James needed His comfort and reassurance. The Master did not fail him.

Because of his faith and his refusal to renounce his faith, James was cast from the battlements of the Temple. Surviving the fall only provided opportunity for the mob to club him to death before his body was torn apart.

JUDAS THADDAEUS (JUDE)

The brother of James the Less, he lived unheralded and little acclaimed, ministering in obscurity. Jude brought the life of a lively and brave young man to Christ. It was Jude who had the last opportunity to seek advice from the Lord before the arrest when he asked: "How is it that You will manifest Yourself to us, and not to the world?" (John 14:22, NKJV).

Jesus responded, "If anyone loves Me, he will keep My word; and My Father will love him, and We will come to him and make Our home with him" (v. 23, NKJV). It is reported that Jude, also known as Thaddaeus, went to Persia and later to Armenia, where he was executed by the reigning monarch.

SIMON

Zeal and even a rebellious nature is the gift that Simon offered to Christ. However, Simon's idealism was greater than his political sense. When the supreme idealism of Jesus Christ was presented to him, he forsook the lesser for the greater. Simon initially expected Christ to restore the kingdom to Israel. He kept this thought until Christ announced, after the Resurrection, that the apostles were not to know the time and season of the restoration of Israel.

In fact, Jesus firmly removed that issue from the consideration of the apostles with the commandment to go into all the world and disciple all nations until the end of the age. Simon became gentle and loving through his association with Jesus and the other disciples. He was dedicated to proclaiming the life of Christ. Eusebius in his *Church History* tells of the exploits of this robust disciple. Simon did this with ardor and enthusiasm, even though it cost him his life. Eusebius says that Simon went to Egypt and Africa and then across the Mediterranean Sea and landed upon the English shore. After preaching the gospel, Simon joins Thaddaeus in Persia and is sawn asunder there.

JUDAS

The controversial Judas joined the other apostles in preparation to meet with Jesus. Jesus saw worthwhile qualities in Judas. He put him in charge of the money and travel accommodations as the group moved about Galilee. Judas didn't seem to understand what Jesus was trying to do and what His mission in life was. Jesus warned Judas many times not to place too much hope and confidence in money or fame or the things of this world. But he seemed to disregard the warnings.

Judas didn't take Jesus' warnings about His impending death very seriously. Judas was a Zealot and hoped that Jesus would restore Israel to its rightful place of honor and glory. Perhaps he didn't think that Jesus would really die before restoring Israel. After all, he had seen Jesus perform many miracles. However, Judas made his own decisions in the light of his own desires, but it was at a terrible cost. For a life lived and gained for self is lost.

(The Twelve are now in the Upper Room.)

The Twelve anxiously await their Master.

The 12 men closest to Jesus—they are all together with the same heartache, the same memories, the same anxieties.

The Master joins them . . .

Jesus begins washing their feet. Peter refuses, but the Master enjoins him to let Him, reminding him that unless He washes Peter's feet that Peter will have no place with Him in the Kingdom.

As they sit down to the table, Jesus tells them of His coming death. But they do not understand His words. He senses their troubled hearts and speaks words of comfort.

Jesus says, "Let not your heart be troubled; you believe in God, believe also in Me. . . . I go to prepare a place for you. And if I go . . . , I will come again and receive you to Myself; that where I am, there you may be also" (John 14:1-3, NKJV).

The disciples become frightened.

As they eat Jesus "took bread, gave thanks and broke it, and gave it to them, saying, 'This is my body given for you; do this in remembrance of me'" (Luke 22:19).

Then "he took the cup, saying, 'This cup is the new covenant in my blood, which is poured out for you'" (v. 20).

Then He startles them with these words, "I tell you the truth, one of you will betray me—one who is eating with me" (Mark 14:18).

Stung by this news, each one frantically begins searching his own heart, saying, "Surely not I?" (v. 19).

"Is it I?" asks Judas. Jesus says to him, "You have said it" (Matt. 26:25, NKJV).

Rejecting the Master's offer of repentance, Judas leaves his place at the table vacant and goes out into the night to arrange for his deed.

Eleven confused and bewildered men continue with the meal. The pulse of the remaining disciples speeds as they sit unbelieving that anyone could betray their beloved Master.

(*The lights can dim. You may close the program however you desire.*

This may be a time to ponder what choices might be made by those seated around the congregation. It is an opportunity to partake of the eucharistic feast and reflect upon what Christ has done.)

APPENDIX 7

Good Friday Worship

Sample Service

Good Friday Candlelight Service

Pianist:

Song Leader:

Worship Leader:

Welcome: You are welcome to this very special service of remembering. At any time, feel free to give verbal praise to God, go to the cross and nail your nail, pray at the altar, hug someone, whatever. This is your service. Most of all, remember: "God so loved the world that he gave his one and only Son, that whoever believes in him shall not perish but have eternal life" (John 3:16).

Hear Ye! Hear Ye!
THE BEST NEWS THAT THE WORLD EVER HAD
CAME FROM A GRAVEYARD NEAR JERUSALEM!

SERVICE ORDER
Prayer

Hymn: "Lead Me to Calvary"

Hymn: "When I Survey"

Scripture: Luke 22:66–23:25

Sharing

Hymn: "Beneath the Cross of Jesus"

Scripture: Luke 23:26-43

Hymn: "At the Cross"

Hymn: "Blessed Redeemer"

Sharing

Hymn: "Wounded for Me"

Scripture: Luke 23:44-56

Special Song: "The Old Rugged Cross"/"At the Cross" Medley

Reading: "The Man on the Center Cross" (Don Adams)

Hymn: "Wonderful Savior"

Closing Prayer

Nailing a Nail into the Cross

Large nails or spikes are given to every person who attends the worship service on Palm Sunday. They are to carry the nails with them during the week and bring them back to the Good Friday service on Friday evening. The hope is that as they are asked why they are carrying such a large nail that they will have opportunity to discuss their faith in the resurrected Savior.

The nails are brought to the Good Friday candlelight service. During the service individuals may come forward and nail their nail into the cross, either nailing some concern, sin, or even prayer to the cross.

Putting Post-Its onto the Cross

Distribute a blank Post-It to everyone who attends worship on Palm Sunday. During the service give them time to write a prayer concern, confess a sin, leave a name of a loved one that they are concerned about, and so forth. At the end of the service invite the congregation to file forward and place their Post-It on a hewn wooden cross that is erected on the platform.

This service could also be used for the Good Friday service, using the Post-Its at the end of the service.

Both of these activities can be very meaningful for the congregation.

Stations of the Cross

(There are many models for a service revolving around the stations of the Cross. The following is meant only as one suggestion. I recommend that you read the narrations with songs placed between each station. Pictures are readily available on the World Wide Web; also several publishers publish packets, complete with the entire service, which may be purchased.)

From the earliest of days, followers of Jesus told the story of his passion, death, and resurrection. When pilgrims came to see Jerusalem, they were anxious to see the sites where Jesus was. These sites become important holy connections with Jesus. Eventually, following in the footsteps of the Lord, along the way of the Cross, became a part of the pilgrimage visit. The stations, as we know them today, came about when it was no longer easy or even possible to visit the holy sites.

The stations of the Cross are 14 stations that review the last few hours of Jesus' life. The celebration of the stations started almost immediately upon the death of Jesus. The stations were set up throughout the city of Jerusalem—going from place to place. From there it was carried to other cities.

Often each city would adopt a station and that would become its focal point. During the great persecutions the stations became a source of great strength for the Church. But also they began to take on new meaning. They moved from the celebration of a historical event to personal devotions. Each station took on a particular meaning for the participant personally. It became far more than remembering an event.

The Context for the Stations

The first point to note is that reflection on the stations of the

Cross is *prayer*. It isn't an intellectual exercise. As one views the stations, the context is their relationship with God. This is more than reading through the text of each of the stations and looking at the pictures, it is an exercise in prayer. This is an invitation to enter into a gifted faith experience of who Jesus is. It becomes prayer when one opens his or her heart to be touched, and it leads one to express his or her response in prayer.

The second thing to remember is that this is an *imaginative* exercise. Its purpose is not a historical examination of "what really happened" on that day in history. It's about something far more profound. This is an opportunity to use this long-standing Christian prayer to let Jesus touch hearts deeply by showing the depth of His love. These exercises can allow one to imaginatively visualize the "meaning" of His passion and death.

There are several ways that one can participate or lead people through the stations:

- Show the stations as slides and have someone read the context and then with guided prayer lead the congregation through each one. Songs could be sung or played between the slides and readings.

- Create your own "path" of stations and allow people to take their own tour.

The Stations Described

Station 1: Jesus is condemned to death

As Isaiah prophesied, You had done nothing evil nor spoken any word of treachery, yet You were condemned to die. Lord, You willingly accepted Your condemnation, Your passion and death to make reparation for our sins. Dear Jesus, there is no better way to thank You for the sacrifice You made on our behalf than to do the will of our Father in heaven and not let the unjust judgments of people stop us from loving You or them.

Station 2: Jesus carries His cross

Jesus is made to carry the Cross on which He will die. Lord, if in Your innocence You willingly accepted Your cross on our behalf, give us who are guilty of sin the grace to accept our crosses on behalf of others.

Station 3: Jesus falls for the first time

As a man, Lord, how could You not have fallen? Your flesh was torn, Your forehead cut and bleeding, Your body ached from the blows suffered; You were weakened by the loss of blood. They laid the full weight of the Cross upon Your shoulders. That You fell to the ground was no surprise, but that You got up and made Your way to Calvary was evidence of Your infinite love for us. Lord, help us to bear our burdens . . . our crosses . . . out of love for You and those we encounter in this life.

Station 4: Jesus meets His mother

All of us have suffered with loved ones during their times of pain and misfortune. But how can any of us ever appreciate the pain and anguish Your mother suffered when she looked into Your eyes, as only a mother can, and felt Your pain? She knew You were the Son of God, but that knowledge did not lessen her sorrow and distress at that moment, for, like us, she was only human. As Mary stood by You, Jesus, although helpless, give us the grace to support our suffering brothers and sisters, if we do nothing more than quietly stand by their side at times when they need us most.

Station 5: Simon the Cyrene helps Jesus carry His cross

Lord, from what we know of Simon, he came to Jerusalem to celebrate the feast of Passover—not to help carry Your cross. He must have resisted when the soldiers forced him to help You. But when he felt the weight of the cross in his hands and drew close to You, he forgot his fears and embarrassment; no longer did the soldiers and the hostile crowd concern him. All he wished to do was help You with

Your burden. Like Simon, Lord, give us the grace to overcome our fears and embarrassment, and reach out to all who need our help, no matter who they might be.

Station 6: Veronica wipes the face of Jesus

Veronica didn't know You, Lord. She may have only seen You this one time. Carrying Your cross like a common criminal and the object of ridicule and scorn, what else could she have thought, but that You had committed some serious crime. But she also must have seen You as a suffering human being, for she reached out to You in sympathy and friendship. Give us this same strength and courage, Lord, to go out to those who are scorned by others to make them know there is love in this world.

Station 7: Jesus falls for the second time

Once again, You fall under the weight of the Cross. Who would have blamed You if You gave up at that moment? You had already suffered more than most men do in a lifetime. But You didn't give up . . . You had a purpose . . . our salvation . . . and so in spite of the pain You were suffering and were yet to suffer, You continued to struggle on Your way to the Cross. May Your example of love and obedience to the will of Your Father be the example we need to overcome adversity and pain as we, too, struggle to do the will of God, our Father.

Station 8: Jesus speaks to the women of Jerusalem

Lord, You loved so much that, in spite of the injustice, humiliation, suffering, and pain You were enduring, You took time to comfort those in need. Jesus, help me get by my own problems and see the problems of others; help me overlook the indifference shown me as I show my concern for others; and help me come out of myself and reach out to those in need in witness of my love for You.

Station 9: Jesus falls for the third time

How difficult it must have been for You to continue on Your way to Your crucifixion after You fell for the third time. How did You muster the strength to get up one more time? But somehow You did! As we strive to do the will of God the Father, never let us give up— no matter how difficult it may be, for we are not only striving for our own salvation but for the salvation of all those You place before us.

Station 10: Jesus is stripped of His garments

Lord, You let them throw you to the ground and strip You of Your garments. Although You had the power to stop them, You suffered this humiliation in silence. Jesus, may I in times of pride and independence remember Your example of humility and control, and may this example strip me of my vanity and pride so that I may regain perspective and think less of myself and more of others.

Station 11: Jesus is nailed to the Cross

Man's inhumanity to man was never more evident than when the soldiers literally nailed You to the Cross as if You, too, were nothing but another piece of wood. How could a human being inflict such torturous pain on another human being? And yet they did and, unfortunately, still do. Lord, may Your acceptance of the pain of the Cross inspire me to actively work to prevent such pain . . . whether mental or physical . . . from being inflicted on another human being.

Station 12: Jesus dies on the Cross

It is over! Your Father's will is done. As Isaiah prophesied, because You surrendered yourself to death and were counted among the wicked, You shall take away the sins of many and win pardon for their offenses. And because You drank from the cup of obedience, You won salvation for us. We thank You, Lord, and ask that You give us the grace to obediently put our Father's will before that of our own.

Station 13: Jesus is taken down from the Cross

You willed to have Your dead body taken down from the Cross so that You might rise again from the grave in testimony of Your power over death. As bitter as that moment must have been for Mary, Your mother, and all those who took Your body from the Cross, it was a moment that had to be experienced in order for Your victory, and ours, to have been won. Help us to suffer moments of death with the knowledge and belief that we, too, and all who believe in You will be victorious over death as well.

Station 14: Jesus is laid in the tomb

Lord, there is a finality associated with burials that, too often, blinds us from our belief that the soul never dies. May Your tomb be a constant reminder to us that as we die to one life, we are born to another.

Final Slide—Face of the Risen Lord (optional)

Lord, I have relived Your suffering and pain as I have accompanied You on Your way to Calvary and Your death upon the Cross. Let me also through the merits of Your sacrifice share in the glory of Your resurrection.

APPENDIX 8

Readings and Poems

This Man Called Jesus
Through the Eyes of Salome
A One-Person Dramatic Presentation*

I shall never forget my first impression of the man of Nazareth. I heard quite a commotion outside. It was clear that my husband, Zebedee, was angry at something. His thundering voice easily penetrated the walls of our home and pounded into the kitchen where I stood. This was not an uncommon experience, as my husband was well known for his explosive temperament. I decided to ignore it and went about my daily task of overseeing the preparation of breakfast. But after a few minutes of prolonged outbursts, I decided I should investigate.

Not wanting to appear brash by intruding on my husband's affairs, I pretended to busy myself with the grain at the hand mill outside. It was close enough to the men for me to be able to listen inconspicuously. My two sons, James and John, were conversing with a stranger. Intrigue was written into their faces; they seemed to be pondering an important decision. Zebedee, on the other hand, was the intruder to the scene. He was not pondering anything. He was angry—VERY angry. My sons, being of like temperament, only added to the confusion.

---

*© 1979 Ann R. Waller. Used by permission.

"You must be mad!" Zebedee bellowed, his face reddening and his neck veins protruding. "No sons of mine will go wandering around the country like no-good bums. You will stay here with your family and earn an honest living in the trade of your father. I have built this business with my bare hands. Success comes only with brow sweat and calluses. If you dare to . . . ."

"Father, you must understand this is a higher calling . . . ," interrupted James.

"Understand? I *understand* that it is the obligation of Jewish sons to obey their fathers. The fishing business may not be sweet smelling, but it is a respectable way to provide for my family. It has been my dream to establish a business of such high caliber that my sons would be proud to assume the responsibility of its leadership. Now that I have achieved a fine fleet with many servants, my sons wish to walk away to tour the country and follow a man they know little about."

James and John both looked toward Jesus with exasperation. They had run out of approaches.

"I will make them fishers of *men*, if they follow me," was his only reply.

What could be so different about this religious radical? Within a few minutes of his arrival, he threatened Zebedee's lifetime dream for his sons, and the security of our family. How could his appeal come close to, much less overpower, the traditional ties between a Jewish father and his sons?

After all, we were good Jews. We did not follow the law in detail, as some advised. But we made our sacrifices regularly and kept the law as best we could. John even followed the religious leader, John the Baptist, and had been on a few short journeys with him. But it had not interfered with his vocation, his life's work. This man seemed to be asking for much more, for a lifetime commitment that would alter their whole lifestyle. And not from just one, but from both of our sons!

I began to tremble, anticipating the consequences of a scattered family and defiant sons. It was all I could do to try and remain poised and uninvolved.

Then, as they continued their discussion, the stranger shifted enough so that I could see his full countenance for the first time. He was hardly distinguishable from other men in physical appearance. His structure was tall and muscular. His black hair was parted in the middle and flowed in even waves to his shoulders. It framed his golden brown complexion with simple beauty. His black mustache merged smoothly into his full beard. Dark eyes at once penetrated the object of his gaze, stirring in them a confusion of spontaneous love and . . . careful reservation.

It wasn't until then that I also noticed his manner was strikingly different from that of my husband and my sons. Of the four men, he alone was calm and confident of his position in the midst of this turmoil. I have never before or since seen such a combination of love and authority, tenderness and strength. I wanted to run and hide but at the same time I desired to know him, to learn from him, to be guided by him.

Instinctively, I knew there could be no secrets from this man. My attention was snapped back to the conversation. "We will go," James and John both agreed.

In a few eternity-moments, the decision had been made. My sons were defying their father, denying their present lifestyle, and leaving their inheritance. I was stunned.

The next few weeks and months were not easy. It was difficult enough trying to handle my own confusion and disappointments, much less deal with my husband's vocal indignation and his silent heartbreak. Where had we gone wrong?

But being a mother, concerned for the well-being of her children regardless of the path they have chosen, I convinced Zebedee we could survive their decision. He agreed to reserve final judgment until we found out more about this stranger.

It was not long until we began hearing reports of this man called Jesus. He seemed to challenge the security of people wherever he went. James and John sent word of their activities and location whenever possible. Several times they journeyed through or near Bethsaida, enabling us to visit with them. We even traveled around to see them and to listen to Jesus as much as time and money allowed.

The more I was exposed to Jesus and his teachings, the more I was impressed with him. If our sons were to leave home to wander around the country, I was glad it was to be with a man such as this. Zebedee, however, remained unimpressed and aloof.

Since I was able to travel more than my husband, I took advantage of every opportunity to hear this radical teacher. He was so different from the other priests and teachers. Love and mercy were more important to him than justice and the law. He performed many miracles—not fancy tricks with objects, but he healed people. He gave sight and health and life to the poor as well as the rich. But it wasn't just his teachings and miracles—it was his manner, his life that embodied all that he said. You could not know this man for long without loving him . . . or hating him. His truths were straightforward yet complicated, obvious yet disguised. Slowly, but decisively, I believed. He *made* a believer of me by virtue of his authority and love. But did I dare to believe this was the long-awaited Messiah, the promised one who would rise up and deliver us into freedom from our oppressors?

Yes, I eventually believed this, too. Our sons had become very close to him and twice they witnessed the voice of God declaring that this man Jesus was indeed the Son of God. At last . . . the Messiah!

When we found out that he was a common laborer, a carpenter, in his early years, it hardly seemed possible. We even heard that he had been born in a stable! Surely the Son of God could have made his entrance into the world more elaborately. But, nonetheless, I believed. I supported him financially and verbally. The details of when and how he was going to set up his kingdom still remained a mystery. But it was exciting to think that we could be a part of the overthrow of Rome and the reign of the Son of God! I even asked Jesus one time if James and John could rule with him in his kingdom. He said he did not have the power to decide that. It was up to his Father. This discussion caused some argument among the disciples. So Jesus told them that whoever would be great in the kingdom should be servant to all. What an odd combination—power and servitude!

Then in the last six months or so, James and John noticed that Jesus became more intensely serious. He began talking of "little time," and his body and soul became weighed down with preoccupation. Perhaps soon, Jesus would make his move to establish his kingdom. But his mood was puzzling—quiet and subdued—nothing at all how one would picture the Messiah ready to conquer his foes!

It was the time of the feast of the Passover. I had come to Jerusalem to participate in this important celebration. It commemorated God's goodness to us in sparing our forefathers from the plague of death. I did not learn many of the details of the next few days until much later. The commotion of the hordes of people visiting Jerusalem for the Passover hid much of the activity of Jesus' evil enemies.

Jesus' mother, Mary, had also come for the Passover. We were both staying with a family of believers there. As Mary and I were preparing for the coming Sabbath, a neighborhood child ran into the courtyard of the home where we were staying.

"Jesus has been arrested," she sputtered. "I was playing near Pilate's court when I saw a huge crowd moving down the street. I saw Roman soldiers pushing a man toward the courtyard. I climbed upon a wall nearby to catch a glimpse of the captured criminal. But it was Jesus! Why would they want to arrest *him*? He was so kind even to us children."

I threw a frightened glance at Mary. We clutched each other for support.

The wide-eyed child continued, "I stayed a little while longer. Pilate brought Jesus out to the crowd. He wanted to let Jesus go. But many men were there who shouted and chanted to 'crucify him.' They were very angry. I got scared and ran home. Mother said I should come tell you."

I couldn't speak. I couldn't move. Fear ran its chilling course through my veins. Where were my sons? Where were the rest of the apostles? Were they not armed in case such a thing as this should happen? Were they arrested, too?

"We must go," Mary whispered dryly.

"No, Mary. This must be left to the men." Revolution could be bloody. It did not seem things were as they should be, but surely the Messiah could handle the situation no matter how bleak it appeared.

"But . . . he is . . . my son," she stated, her face now drained of its color.

"All right, Mary. We shall investigate as best we can. Perhaps the child has mistaken another man for Jesus."

It sounded hollow, filled only with the air of simulated hope.

We hurried down the cobblestone streets, only to find Pilate's courtyard all but deserted. Two guards attending the palace entrance were the only ones in sight. But a few people were still in the streets. We grabbed a frightened young girl by the shoulders. "Where is Jesus? Where have they taken him?"

Her eyes refused to meet ours. "To be crucified," she murmured.

We hastened on, our feet chattering against the cobblestone streets. It just could not be so! This was not insurrection or revolution! It was not army against army! It was many men against one man—a cold strategy of murder. If Jesus could not free himself of a handful of soldiers, how could he possibly take on the whole of the Roman troop in Jerusalem? Or . . . was he yet to bring forth his brilliant display of power in the midst of insurmountable odds?

We managed to catch up with the crowd as they approached the Gennath Gate near the foot of Golgotha. We maneuvered our way to the center of the group. I found John there, helplessly watching the ritual proceeding. He said the other disciples were scattered. It had all happened so fast and with such finality. Strangely enough Jesus had not permitted them to protect him. Jesus had spoken to them of death in the last few days, but it was difficult to piece it all together. It didn't make sense. How could he die and yet establish his kingdom?

[If a shorter reading is desired, as for Communion or a devotional, this can be the beginning with the following introductory line. Otherwise omit it.]

[I, Salome, mother of James and John, give this account of our Lord.]

It was the third hour. The soldiers were driving the nails into the hands and feet of Jesus. If the feet were nailed full-length and close to the foot of the cross, the criminal died quickly. So it was the Roman custom to push the feet upward on the cross and nail them there so the condemned man could put his weight on this nail wound and push himself upward to breathe. This made possible only a painful extension of doomed existence. A suitable agony for a guilty criminal . . . an unspeakable torture for innocent flesh. I buried my head in John's breast, unable to watch. The cry of metal to metal and metal to flesh and wood pierced the frantic silence. The cross was erected and jilted into its hole with a nauseating thud . . .

The crowd was a curious mixture, overbalanced by the presence of many priests and religious teachers. Some of them began to add their proud interjections to the growing jeers of the crowd.

"He saved others, but he can't save himself! Let this Christ, this 'King of the Jews,' come down now from the cross, that we may see and believe," one called.

My mind was whirling. I was at once horrified, enraged, confused. The situation was out of control. "Yes, Lord! NOW is the moment to annihilate your enemies! Destroy these evil ones! Rise up and conquer them! There is still time!"

It was noontime, the sixth hour. Three hours had passed. Jesus was passively accepting this horrible sacrilege.

Upon seeing his mother there and John nearby, Jesus informed his mother, "Here is your son." And to John, he admonished, "Here is your mother." It was all so final, as if his death were certain.

Then suddenly the sky grew black. There was thunder, but no storm. The earth was crying out in objection to the desecration of this holy man. "Now, Lord, NOW! Rise up and establish your kingdom while their eyes are dulled with darkness." But still no movement was seen on the center cross.

Three more agonizing hours crept by. Jesus moved to gather the strength and breath to speak. Forcing his weight on the nail-wound in his feet, he groaned, "My God, my God, why have you forsaken me?" He paused. His countenance changed from defeat to triumph. With a loud cry of "It is finished!" his breath ceased.

"Oh, my Lord and my God! Is it really finished? Is this the end of it all? This is the death of a criminal, a traitor, a blasphemer! How has everything been completed?"

Or did Jesus try to gather his forces of supernatural aid only to find God had turned his back on his precious son? What is the meaning of this? It was absurd.

Unless . . . this man of mysterious magnetism could have not only deluded a large number of followers, but in fact, deluded himself in the process. We had *so* believed in Jesus as the Messiah. Now hope was dead. Future, nonexistent. Only the present, oppressive blackness remained.

We turned, advising Mary to leave with us, and return to our friend's home and rest. I could not continue to gaze upon the still form on the middle cross. I had loved him as a son. I had believed in him as the Messiah! All was lost, no matter what the explanation.

But Mary insisted, so we followed Joseph of Arimathea to see that the body of her son was laid to rest in a borrowed tomb. Afterwards, we stumbled the blurred and wavering path home. The preparation of the spices and perfumes was a necessary priority. So we performed this morbid duty and dropped into our beds, isolated in our own grief-stricken solitudes. We could not complete his proper burial the next day since it was the Sabbath, so we rested. Actually, we only rested in the sense that we refrained from working.

Early the next morning, we took the spices to the tomb. I still could not believe what had happened. Few words were exchanged between us. It just didn't seem possible that a man filled with so much love and depth could have deceived us so. However, I somehow felt an intangible, unexplainable sense of loyalty and obligation to this man. One cannot stop loving in an instant, even in a moment of great disappointment. He must at least be given a proper burial.

We approached the place of the tomb solemnly, respectfully. But as soon as we reached the level of the tomb, we could see the huge stone that had sealed the entrance had been moved aside. We rushed inside but could not find the body of Jesus. Suddenly two men in brilliant robes stood beside us. Frightened, we bowed to them. They reached to lift us up.

"Why do you look for the living among the dead? He is not here! He has risen! Remember how he told you while he was still with you in Galilee: 'the Son of Man must be delivered into the hands of sinful man, be crucified, and on the third day be raised again.'"

We remembered!

"Oh, my God! My Lord! He is risen! He was—He is—the Messiah! Hope is reborn! Joy is complete!"

Only God, or the Son of God, could conquer death.

Some were skeptical. But in the next several weeks Jesus appeared to many and few could remain unconvinced. It took much time for the myriad implications of what took place to come into focus. But THIS ONE THING WE KNEW: the Messiah had come! He had conquered death, and prepared the way for us to enter his heavenly kingdom. PRAISE HIS HOLY NAME FOREVER AND EVER! Amen.

The Cross*

W. Don Adams

I had become a hated thing,
A thing of pain and death,
A mark of shame and agony,
Of all majesty bereft.

I stood there on that lonely hill;
My shadow marked a city wall
And cast a pall of hopelessness
Wherever it did fall.

I once had graced a mountain side
A cedar tall and straight;
But now I stood in loneliness
Outside that city gate.

Ax-men had felled my sturdy trunk
And trimmed me bough and limb;
They hewed me to a mighty beam
With crossbar neat and trim.

They hauled me down to Pilate's court
And threw me in the pile.
'Twas from there they bound me to His back
Tormenting Him all the while.

A man named Joseph lifted me from
His fallen form and helped Him to His feet
He said, "Friend, lead on, I pray,
I will carry this load, my strength is meet."

---

*Used by permission.

At last we reached Golgotha's crest;
The soldiers laid me on the ground;
Then they bound Him to my cross arm.
They took His seamless robe and all else they found.

I felt the hammer blows as nails
Pierced both hands and feet.
His precious Blood wet my drying wood;
Rough hands lifted me with my load; the cruel act complete.

They set me in a carved out niche
Atop Calvary's lonely mount.
The taunting jeers and wagging heads
Were more than one could count.

I heard Him speak as He looked on high,
"Father, forgive them, they know not what they do."
I shuddered when I heard Him say,
"Father, I have paid the price, I am through."

The lightning flashed! The thunder rolled!
The rock on which I stood all but gave way,
The clouds grew dark and wind swept,
The night blocked out the light of day.

The soldier fell upon his knees
And cried aloud, "This truly was the Son of God" he said.
Then, amid his sobs,
"But now He is dead."

Thus proving the truth of
That condemning plaque above His head,
"This is the Son of God,"
By Pilate's hand it said.

The angry mob slunk off
In guilty fear;
Only a few women and a lad
Stood near.

Then came the mighty
Thrust of the Roman spear,
Just to prove Him truly dead
Beyond any lingering doubt or fear.

Blood and water gushed out upon the ground;
He died of a broken heart by His own will.
The wind had laid, no bird made sound,
The silence was great, it was so still.

In the dusk of the oncoming night
Came Joseph, who had born me up the hill,
With Nicodemus his friend;
They had begged Pilate for His body with all their will.

Now with love and gentleness
They pulled the nails and let Him down.
It was so dark and still,
No spark of hope was found.

They wrapped Him in a burial robe
And laid Him in a new-hewn tomb;
Then rolled a stone across the door,
Sealed it with the governor's ring—Oh, the gloom!

That night-so dark!
No creature stirred,
No rushing wind.

The day dawned dark
And full of chill—
I stood alone
Upon the wretched hill.

The next night passed
Without hope or cheer.
Then it came—
So strong and clear!

The trumpet sound, the angel shout!
The stone rolled back from off the door!
Forth came He whom Death's grim chains
Could hold no more!

"He lives! He lives!"
Went forth the cry.
"He lives! He lives!
No more to die!"

So around the world was heard
The glory of His wondrous word;
Even unto this day this same
Salvation message is heard.

Now I stand on cathedral walls
And the mountain peaks, oh, so tall;
My light shines out to lift the souls of men
From out sin's dreadful, crushing pall,

I am the means by which man's selfish self meets death;
That the Holy Spirit of Christ may enter and reign within.
I am the symbol of Saving Grace—
the sign men's souls can be saved from sin.

My cedar form long since decayed;
My native hills made bare.
I have been immortalized—
The symbol of faith and prayer.

The Man on the Center Cross*
W. Don Adams

My beloved Claudia, from your adoring Arius, greetings:
I write to you to express my deep love,
Also to relieve my troubled mind of the events of this day.
I know that, this day, I stood in the presence of Deity from above.
I saw the Man on that center cross.

Ten years have I served in the Roman legions;
Death has been my constant companion; to it, I have become hard.
I have seen men die in battle, in the arena, and on the cross.
No sentimental visionary will make Centurion in the governor's
    guard.
But I saw this day the Man on the center cross.

At about the third hour of the day, I received orders to
Take a man from the guard-house at the Pavement, the court
of Pilate, to Calvary, for He had been sentenced to die on the tree.
Two others were to die this day; however, this Man, the most
    infamous, so the report,
Was to die on the center cross.

As the custom is, we laid His cross on His bleeding back
And started the long trail to Calvary's crest.
Before long He fell beneath the load; the heavy cross clattered
on the Cobblestone road; it was evident He needed more than rest,
the Man carrying the center cross.

Standing by the roadside was a man of dark skin and great strength.
I touched him on the shoulder with the flat of my spear,

*W. Don Adams. © 1992. Used by permission

And motioned toward the cross that lay on the roadway there.
With a scowl, he reached for the cross, not out of compassion but of
    fear.
With one hand, he lifted the Man that lay beneath the center cross.

In that moment their eyes met;
The harsh lines on the big man's face softened without delay.
The scowl melted like snowflakes on a warm, sunny day.
"Gladly," he said, "will I carry the cross all of the way."
A smile of love crossed the face of Him who on the center cross was
    to hang.

When we reached the top of Calvary hill the others were there.
The two thieves cursed and screamed as they were thrown
On their crosses and the nails driven through their hands.
Their crosses were lifted and dropped in their sockets; the curses
    turned to a moan.
Quietly stood the Man by the center cross.

There was no struggle as the soldiers laid Him on the cross;
It was as though He yielded himself willingly, death to meet.
There was no cursing or screaming, only a low moan,
As the nails were driven through not only His hands, but also his
    feet.
The soldiers then lifted the Man on the center cross.

Hanging there, obviously in very great pain, He did something very
    strange.
He lifted His eyes toward heaven and prayed,
"Father, forgive them, for they know not what they do."
In my hard heart there was a stir; there the words of that prayer have
    stayed,
The prayer of the Man on the center cross.

Beneath the three crosses and out in front of them, there was a
Motley mob of Jews, made up of those caught in the mire
Of the sects and cults of their religion; most of the time they fought
Among themselves, but now they had a common object of their ire,
The Man on the center cross.

They shouted insults and jibes, something about, "If thou
Be the Christ, come down from the cross and we will believe."
I don't know what it was all about.
Beneath the crosses, and to one side of the mob, stood four women
 who would not leave.
They wept as they gazed at the Man on the center cross.

The Man on the center cross, seeing them standing there, called to
One of them saying, "Woman, behold, your son." A young man
Standing with them moved up close to the woman addressed from
 the tree.
"Son," He continued, "Behold, your mother." The woman
was taken into the arms of the young man.
All this as they lovingly looked at the Man on the center cross.

It was the sixth hour, the Man on the center cross groaned, as if
In great mental torment, and darkness began to fall.
It was not so much that the darkness came,
As it was that the light withdrew, and darkness covered all—
Even the Man on the center cross.

The two thieves had been joining in the reviling, but now,
The one on the right said to the other something like this,
"That is enough; do you not fear God, being in the same
 condemnation?
We are getting our just due, but this Man has done nothing amiss."
Turning to the Man on the center cross, he cried.

"Lord, remember me when thou comest into thy kingdom."
The Man on the center cross replied, "This day shall you walk with
  me
In the inner garden of the palace of the King of Kings."
The darkness deepened, the air was permeated with evil causing all
  courage to flee,
As the blackness swirled around the Man on the center cross.

The ninth hour approached, the darkness grew even blacker.
Then, from the center cross, came the cry, "My God, my God,
why hast thou forsaken me?"
The evil storm seemed to intensify; out of the blackness
Came another cry, "It is finished!" The battle was won, His soul was
  free.
Light began to dispel the darkness around that center cross.

Thunder rolled and a lightning bolt flashed striking the temple
  mount,
As Calvary was rocked by an earthquake shock.
He bowed His head and quietly said, "Father, into Thy hand I
  commend my spirit."
I pulled off my helmet and dropped on my knees; these things my
  very being had rocked.
I cried of the Man on the center cross, "This is the Son of God."

The Jews left the hilltop beating their breasts.
Because the Jewish Sabbath was drawing nigh,
I, with my soldiers, had to make sure that the men on the crosses
Really were dead and off of the crosses, with the Jewish law to
  comply—
Even the Man on the center cross.

The men on the other crosses were yet alive,
So their legs with a mallet were broken.
The man on the center cross, I knew, was already dead;
To fulfill my order I thrust my spear into His side, just as a token.
Behold! Blood and water gushed form the Man on the center cross.

A man named Joseph, who came from Arimathea, begged
Of Pilate the body of the Man on the center cross.
With a friend named Nicodemus, he tenderly took it down,
Wound it in fine linen and laid it in a tomb, mourning all the while
    their loss.
In my mind I still see that Man on the center cross.

Claudia, my dear, I don't know the meaning of all this;
Pilate's placard read, "Jesus of Nazareth, the King of the Jews."
Yet they reviled and cursed Him and wanted Him dead.
As I listened and watched, as the day unfolded, I could choose
Only one name, The Son of God, for the Man on the center cross.
Your Adoring,
Arias

Postscript—Claudia! He lives! He lives!
This is the first day of the week and the Tomb
Is empty! He appeared unto a man named Peter, to one of
Those women that stood by His tree and in my heart's innermost
    room,
Oh, Claudia! He appeared to me!
This Man from the center cross.

The Twelve Steps of Redemption*

Rob Robinson

Good Friday
Twelve steps of utmost love
Twelve steps of utter loneliness, despair, betrayal,
Agony
    all in the name of love . . .

Step One
    the Garden
    His friends are sleeping,
    As He prays
    The entire scene to come unfolds for Him
    Every approaching moment
        of torture and pain
    So vivid, so clear
    He sweats the sweat of agony, blood,
    And yet, His response?
        "Not my will, but Thine."

Step Two
    An intimate follower who has seen
    The miracles, the love,
    Heard the imagery of heavenly thoughts
    For three years
    Betrays Him
    With a kiss.

---

*Rob Robinson (April 11, 2004). Used by permission.

Step Three

> Arrested by Temple guards and officials
> Brought to the home of the High Priest of Israel
> Abused, beaten, mocked
> By those who should know a true
> High Priest when He stands before them,
> But they don't.

Step Four

> Though everyone else betrays you
> I never will, Peter declared,
> But Jesus, silent lamb in Caiaphas' court,
> Watches as this loyal, simple fisherman
> Denies Him,
> Not once, not twice,
> But three times.

Step Five

> They are the ruling body
> Of the Chosen People,
> But with He who chose them
> Standing before their questioning gaze
> The leaders of the Children of Israel
> In the very presence of their true King
> Condemn Him
> To die.

Step Six

> What is truth? Pilate asks,
> But does he really care to know,
> For Truth stands silently before him
> And he knows it not,
> Nor recognizes Truth's solemn gaze.

Step Seven

The King of Kings stands silently
Before this false king of Israel, Herod,
No words can enlighten
This worldly ruler whose soul is so dark,
Jesus is mocked by
This mockery of a king.

Step Eight

Punished to the brink of death
A Roman whip that ripped the flesh
Making His back and ribs a crisscrossed mess
Of open wounds
That spoke of the authority
Of a governor working more to appease
Than for justice,
Which only God can truly give.

Step Nine

Two men, one a condemned murderer,
One a backwoods teacher
A worker of miracles, who barely stood now
The red fluid of His life dripping, soaking through
His garments,
"Choose," the governor proclaimed to the mob,
"Barabbas," they exclaimed
And traded a murderer for a lamb
To be crucified.

Step Ten

Staggering under the load of a wooden beam
    exhausted, bleeding, in agony,
    prodded by faceless guards duty bound,

    past crowds, in shock, beholding the good rabbi
      how could this be?
Tortured streets, mobs, Simon the Cyrene forced to lend a hand
The Villa de la Rosa,
      The way to death.

Step Eleven
    Stripped of dignity, stretched in agony
    Upon a cross of wood,
    Arms held by ropes
    As large, cruel spikes were driven, methodical
    Hammer blow, by hammer blow
      in and through
      the wrist
      the feet
      blood spurting all the while
    Conscious on the raw edge of pain
    He is lifted on the cross
      slammed down
      then the gasp for air
      the push and pull on the nails
      in hands and feet
      searing agony up and down to breathe
      slump to relieve the shooting pain on the feet
      but the lungs begin to collapse and fill
      with water and blood
      push up again
        gasp for air
    Crucifixion.

Step Twelve
    The eyes begin to swim in a sea of red
    There is no world but pain and suffering

Somewhere below the earthly mother,
Some friends,
Some foes,
All are forgiven,
The end is near,
At last it has been done,
"Telestelai," He murmurs,
Paid in full,
Sin and death
Have met their master
And we are
Redeemed.

Simple Cross of Wood*
Rob Robinson

We've prettied it up, haven't we?
That simple cross of wood,
With silver and gold, with intricate hues
That hide the scars of Holy Blood,
We've prettied up your message, too,
Concentrating on a God of love—
But it was the God of justice
Who sent to sinful earth from heaven above,

A Son to bear all sins and shame,
To be scourged like a common thief,
To be counted with the transgressors,
To conquer all death and grief.

Lord, you bled, you hurt,
You felt deep pain, as your
Children denied your very name,
We laughed at you, at infinite love,
We scorned the innocent, holy Dove.

It won't be the sparkling hues
Of delicate stained glass that will save me,
It won't be a shining silver cross,
Or padded pews, or carpeted aisles,
Or handing out clever gospels for free.

*Used by permission.

No, no, my friend, it will be the cross,
The bloodstained, wooden tree,
The sin that died, the Savior that rose,
My whiteness when He redeems me.

Thank you for that pain, my Lord,
For the whippings and the awful suffering
That you took on for worthless me,
Thank you that I have gained
All that once was lost,
When standing in the shadow
Of that ugly-beautiful, loving, wooden cross.

NOTES

Introduction

1. Barry Liesch, *The New Worship* (Grand Rapids: Baker Books, 2001), 13.

2. Michael Lodahl, *The Story of God* (Kansas City: Beacon Hill Press of Kansas City, 1994), 13.

3. *The Constitution on the Sacred Liturgy. Sacrosanctum Concilium* (Solemnly Promulgated by His Holiness Pope Paul VI on December 4, 1963, par. 102), http://www.vatican.va/archive/hist_councils/ii_vatican_council/documents/vat-ii_const_19631204_sacrosanctum-concilium_en.html.

4. Dennis Bratcher, *The Voice: Christian Resource Institute*. http://www.cresourcei.org/chyear.html.

5. N. T. Wright, *Twelve Months of Sundays: Reflections on Bible Readings, Year C* (Great Britain: Society for Promotion Christian Knowledge, 2000), 3.

6. Justin Martyr, *First Apology*, chap. 67, "Weekly Worship of the Christians" (A.D. 130), Christian Classics Etheral Library, http://www.ccel.org/ccel/schaff/anf01.viii.ii.lxvii.html.

7. James D. Smart, *The Strange Silence of the Bible in the Church* (Philadelphia: Westminster Press, 1976), 24.

8. *Revised Common Lectionary*, Vanderbilt University, http://divinity.library.vanderbilt.edu/lectionary/

Chapter 1

1. Robert E. Webber, ed., *The Complete Library of Christian Worship* (Nashville: Star Song Publishing Group, 1994), 131.

2. The alternate themes are from Webber, *Complete Library of Christian Worship*.

Chapter 2

1. "The Celebration of Christmas," Mother Bedford, http://www.motherbedford.com/Christmas.htm.

Chapter 4

1. Ken Collins, "The Season of Lent," Rev. Ken Collins' Web Site, http://www.kencollins.com/holy-04.htm. See also *The Apostolic Constitutions, an adaptation of the Didascalia Apostorum* (Syria: A.D. 250), Book V, Section III, "On Feast Days and Fast Days," Christian Classics Ethereal Library, http://www.ccel.org/ccel/schaff/anf07.ix.vi.iii.html.

2. Geoffrey Chaucer, "The Parliament of Fowles," lines 309-10, The Online and Medieval Classical Library, http://omacl.org/Parliament/.

Chapter 5

1. *Webster's II New Riverside University Dictionary*, s.v. "Passion."

2. You can obtain a Hagadah, a Jewish worship guide for the seder meal, many places online or through a Jewish synagogue. Amazon.com is a good place to find a modern translation.

3. "Easter Lilies," PLANTanswers, http://plantanswers.tamu.edu/publications/lily/lily.html.

4. "Holy Humor Sunday!" see http://www.fccoshkosh.org/Humor2006.html and http://www.fccoshkosh.org/humor2007.html.

Chapter 6

1. John Paul II, "Dies Domini," No. 37 (Apostolic Letter, July 5, 1998) http://www.vatican.va/holy_father/john_paul_ii/apost_letters/documents/hf_jp-ii_apl_05071998_dies-domini_en.html.

2. Alister McGrath, *Christian Theology: An Introduction*, 3rd ed. (Malden, Mass.: Blackwell, 2001), 251.

3. Sarah Josepha Hale, *American Ladies Magazine* (Editorial, 1863) http://www.bestyears.com/sarah_hale.html.

4. Abraham Lincoln, "Thanksgiving Day Proclamation" (Washington, D.C.: October 3, 1863), http://showcase.netins.net/web/creative/lincoln/speeches/thanks.htm.

BIBLIOGRAPHY

"Apostles and Other Historical Figures of the Early Church," George's Bible Study Notes, http://www.imt.net/~gedison/apostle.html.

Barclay, William. *The Gospel of Matthew*, Vol. 1. The Daily Study Bible Series. Edinburgh: St. Andrews Press, 1956.

Bratcher, Dennis. *The Voice: Christian Resource Institute.* http://www.cresourcei.org/chyear.html.

Buscaglia, Leo. *Seven Stories of Christmas Love.* Thorofare, N.J.: SLACK Inc., 1987.

Chaucer, Geoffrey. "The Parliament of Fowles," lines 309-10. The Online and Medieval Classical Library. http://omacl.org/Parliament/.

Collins, Ken. "The Season of Lent." Rev. Ken Collins' Web Site. http://www.kencollins.com/holy-04.htm.

Constitution on the Sacred Liturgy *SACROSANCTUM CONCILIUM* Solemnly Promulgated by His Holiness Pope Paul VI on December 4, 1963, par. 102. http://www.vatican.va/archive/hist_councils/ii_vatican_council/documents/vat-ii_const_19631204_sacrosanctum-concilium_en.html.

Dix, William "As With Gladness Men of Old" (1860).

"Easter Lilies," PLANTanswers, http://plantanswers.tamu.edu/publications/lily/lily.html.

Hale, Sarah Josepha. *American Ladies Magazine* (Editorial, 1863). http://www.bestyears.com/sarah_hale.html.

John Paul II, "Dies Domini," No. 37 (Apostolic Letter, July 5, 1998). http://www.vatican.va/holy_father/john_paul_ii/apost_letters/documents/hf_jp-ii_apl_05071998_dies-domini_en.html.

Justin Martyr. *First Apology,* chapter 67, "Weekly Worship of the Christians" (A.D. 130). Christian Classics Ethereal Library. http://www.ccel.org/ccel/schaff/anf01.viii.ii.lxvii.html.

Liesch, Barry. *The New Worship.* Grand Rapids: Baker Books, 2001.

Lincoln, Abraham. "Thanksgiving Day Proclamation." Washington, D.C.: October 3, 1863. http://showcase.netins.net/web/creative/lincoln/speeches/thanks.htm.

Lodahl, Michael. *The Story of God.* Kansas City: Beacon Hill Press of Kansas City, 1994.

McGrath, Alister. *Christian Theology: An Introduction,* 3rd ed. Malden, Mass.: Blackwell, 2001.

Olford, Stephen. *The Pulpit and the Christian Calendar: Preaching on Significant Days.* Stephen F. Olford Biblical Preaching Library; Baker Pub Group, 1991.

Renovare. http://www.renovare.org/

Sacred Space. http://www.sacredspace.ie/.

Smart, James D. *The Strange Silence of the Bible in the Church.* Philadelphia: Westminster Press: 1976.

The Apostolic Constitutions, an adaptation of the Didascalia Apostorum (Syria: A.D. 250), Book V, Section III. "On Feast Days and Fast Days." Christian Classics Ethereal Library. http://www.ccel.org/ccel/schaff/anf07.ix.vi.iii.html.

"The Celebration of Christmas." Mother Bedford. http://www.motherbedford .com/Christmas.htm.

The Revised Common Lectionary, a Vanderbilt Library Online Resource. http://www.library.vanderbilt.edu/divinity/lectionary.

"The Search for the Twelve Apostles." BiblePath.Com. http://biblepath.com/ apostles.html.

Webber, Robert E., ed. *The Complete Library of Christian Worship*. Nashville: Star Song Publishing Group, 1994.

Webster's II New Riverside University Dictionary. Boston: Riverside Publishing Company, a Houghton Mifflin subsidiary, 1984.

Wright, N. T. *Twelve Months of Sundays: Reflections on Bible Readings, Year C*. Great Britain: Society for Promoting Christian Knowledge, 2000.

AN INVALUABLE TOOL FOR EVERY PASTOR

This beneficial, adaptable resource helps pastors make every couple's wedding day something special. Perfect for the multi-tasking minister, it outlines every part of the wedding process and includes ideas for a variety of traditional and contemporary ceremony styles. From pre-marital counseling topics to message outlines for unique ceremonies, this all-inclusive manual makes the minister's job of pronouncing two people "husband and wife" easier and even more meaningful.

The Pastor's Wedding Planner
By Stan Toler
ISBN: 978-0-8341-2425-7

Includes:

- Pre-marital counseling topics and questions
- Suggestions for more than 20 different ceremony styles
- Sermon ideas and message outlines on several different themes
- Scripture readings, benedictions, and song suggestions
- Wedding checklists, building policies, shower ideas, and more

BEACON HILL PRESS
OF KANSAS CITY

Available online and wherever books are sold.

It's one thing to want to change—
it's another to know how.

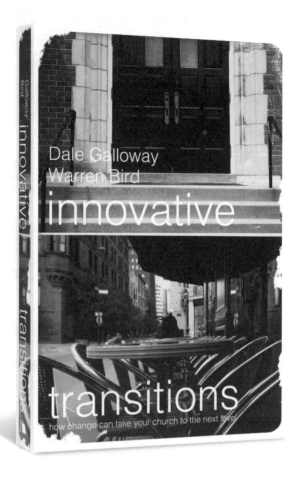

In this inspiring and relevant book, well-known pastor Dale Galloway and church researcher Warren Bird team up to help you transition your church to a healthier, more vibrant, more outwardly focused expression of the Body of Christ. If you're ready to shepherd your church to the next level, their practical methods and innovative examples will show you how to move from where you are to where you need to be.

Innovative Transitions
How Change Can Take Your Church to the Next Level
By Dale Galloway and Warren Bird
ISBN: 978-0-8341-2339-7

BEACON HILL PRESS
OF KANSAS CITY

Available online and wherever books are sold.

"... a spell-binding demonstration of how metaphor, imagery, and verbal cinematography can be used to reach the 21st-century mind."

—*Dr. Darrell Moore, Nazarene Theological Seminary*

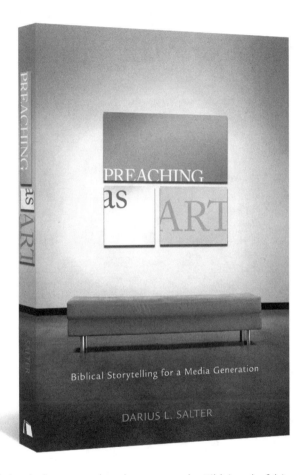

This book shows preachers how to use the Bible's colorful imagery and literary brilliance to celebrate God's amazing story. Darius Salter conveys practical ideas, illustrations, and a variety of media options to help pastors transform their messages into art forms that invite listeners to experience Scripture and encounter God as never before.

PREACHING AS ART
Biblical Storytelling for a Media Generation
By Darius L. Salter
ISBN: 978-0-8341-2359-5

BEACON HILL PRESS
OF KANSAS CITY

Available online and wherever books are sold.

IT'S NOT JUST ABOUT
ARRANGING WORDS—
IT'S ABOUT
CONNECTING GOD
TO HIS PEOPLE.

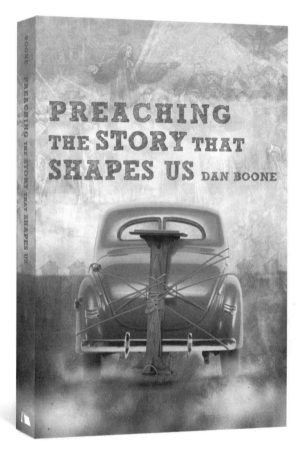

This inspiring text uses scripture, personal narrative, structure, and theological reflection to model the art of storytelling and provide a satisfying, efficient guide to narrative preaching. From using the power of biography to exploring creative ideas for sermon development, it will help you preach engaging, soul-shaping messages using the stories that show us who we are and lead us to who we will be.

Preaching the Story That Shapes Us
By Dan Boone
ISBN: 978-0-8341-2371-7

BEACON HILL PRESS
OF KANSAS CITY

Available online and wherever books are sold.